WEAVING MOONLIGHT

ALSO BY ERICK DUPREE

*Finding the Goddess In Masculine's Spiral:
Men in Community, Ritual, and Service to the Goddess*

Alone In Her Presence: Meditations on the Goddess

Weaving Moonlight

Lunar Mysteries, Meditations, and Magic for the Soul

Erick DuPree

Circle Within Press
Boston

Copyright © 2014 by Erick J. DuPree

All rights reserved. This book or any portion thereof may not be reproduced or used in any manner whatsoever without the express written permission of the publisher except for the use of brief quotations in a book review.

Cover Art: Erick DuPree, design and layout Erick DuPree

*Disclaimer: The activites, ritual, meditation, and advice and statements have not been evaluated by the Food and Drug Administration. These recommendations are not intended to diagnose, treat, cure or prevent any disease.

Printed in the United States of America

First Printing, 2014

ISBN 978-0692284506

Circle Within Press
1213 Freeport Suite 2
Dorchester, MA 02116

To the Moon in all her resplendent glory....

Contents

	Acknowledgments	
	Introduction	11
i	Weaving Moonlight	17

Part I

ii	The New Moon	23
iii	The Waxing Moon	39
iv	The Full Moon	64
v	The Waning Moon	83
vi	The Dark Moon	106

Part II

vii	Drawing Down the Moon	116
viii	A Blue Moon	160
ix	Moon Tides	165
x	Many Moons	172
xi	Healing Moons	188
xii	Moon Signs	195
	Resources	217
	Bibliography	219

The pale Moon dreams

Of being noticed.

The bright Moon dreams

Of being heard.

The new Moon dreams

Of stars in the sky,

to get through

the dark night.

The crescent Moon dreams

of being young forever

Acknowledgements

French philosopher, Simone De Beauvoir once said, "One's life has value so long as one attributes value to the life of others, by means of love, friendship, indignation and compassion." It is within the context of other's greatness, I find myself humbled and indebted. The list of people would be endless, but always first I honor the Great Goddess, who flows in, among, and around us. From Her all things emerge, and unto Her they all return! She continues to bless this journey.

I dedicate this book to the Moon. The luminous and immanent wonder whom has shone radiant beams since the beginning of time. Like many writers, she has inspired this book, the lessons in it and an invitation to find alignment and practice in her beams.

My sisters; Julia, Suzanne, and Katie, and my mother and grandmother. While we may not agree on religion, we agree that to know and to seek truly sets us free.

Many people made this possible, from my beloved colleague in all things magical, YesheRabbit Matthews who continues to inspire me, to my mentors Ivo Dominguez, Jr. and T. Thorn Coyle whom with reflective eyes, inviting me to will, to know, and to dare.

To Starhawk for graciously allowing me to reprint her adaptation of The Charge of the Goddess.

To my teachers, Mariel Freeman, Sue Elkind, Nikki Robinson, Gina Weddle, Kilkenny Tremblay, Jillian Pransky, and Denise Orloff, each who make manifesting the life I want a practice in physical embodiment. Yoga is life, and life should feel like an invitation, never an obligation. Their wisdom is peppered in this book.

Lastly, to my readers! I was plucked from blogging obscurity, and given this incredible platform to offer wisdom. From *Alone in Her Presence* to *Finding the Masculine in Goddess' Spiral*, I am honored that many turn to my writings and workshops to live full lives, in alignment with the universal truth that Love is Still the Law, and that Love is Stronger than Fear!

Thank you, for allowing me into your lives.

Erick DuPree
November 2014

INTRODUCTION

Underneath the starlight
There's a magical feeling so bright
You can't fight the Moonlight
It's gonna get to your heart
— *Diane Warren*

The Moon. She follows me nightly. Sometimes she is full and bright, a buoyant reflection of the self. She is the pallid embers in the night sky, a slow burn in the darkness. She is the fertile crescent of new beginnings, a waxing cradle of possibility, and she is the slivered wane of what might have been. Steadfast and true, the Moon has danced this story for as long as time. Always present, as immanent as the sky itself.

Although we all talk about the Moon, think about the Moon, look up at the Moon, the Moon still remains a mystery. She has been with us since the beginning, and will be for aeons to come. Because of the mystery, the Moon holds a fascination for everyone, and who can help being riveted by the beauty of a full Moon and what the Moon can reveal? The light of the Moon seems to contain a magic all its own, something that we all wish to share in, the allure of the Moon has a place in our hearts, as it did in the hearts of our ancestors.

The Moon has connotations from many wisdom traditions. The word Moon comes from the Greek meaning *measure,* and it is in the measurement, we find celebrations with date specific connections to the Moon.

The ancient Egyptians discovered that although the Moon shape shifted with precision regularity, it did not provide an accurate measure of the seasons. There was always a miscalculation by several days. The regularity of the Moon's ability to shape shift was a way for ancient civilizations to be able to keep time, and the cycles of the Moon were the basis of the earliest calendars. Farmers needed to know when to plant and to harvest, merchants needed to know when to expect to have crops for sale. It was also necessary to have an accurate gauge of the season to be prepared for the annual flooding of the River Nile, none of which could take place without an accurate measure of time. The next calendar designed by the Egyptians was based on solar cycles, which gave them a more accurate measure of time.

There was an early awareness of the Moon's connection to the oceans of the world and the cycles of nature, the Moon affects the creatures of the sea, many of which mate and spawn during particular cycles of the tides. Some fish are easier to catch during the full Moon, birds and animals are all affected during the phase of the full Moon, animals are more active at this time. Ancient civilizations used the Moon to predict weather patterns, and it was likely that was thought to be magic.

There is the legend of the Moon Maiden who collects the wishes and dreams of all living creatures on earth, they are then dropped into a goblet and swirled together before they are sprinkled back on Earth and become dew. The German goddess Frigg is said to live on the Moon spinning the lives of humankind, while the Chinese goddess Ch'ang O stole the potion of immortality from her husband. She drank every drop and flew to the Moon to escape, she now lives there contentedly after being given refuge by the hare who lives on the Moon.

When building a wooden fence you want to last, lay the foundation and set the posts while the Moon is Waning, then wait until the Moon's horns point skyward, you may then lay the lower rail. When the Moon's horns point to Earth the fence can be completed, when building a fence in this way it will be sturdy and last. When the Moon is Waxing hooks for fishing can be set, when the Moon wanes fish by the light of day. If you bow to the new Moon good luck will be yours. To assure an auspicious marriage, marry twenty-four to forty-eight hours after the full Moon, and the Scottish believe that a wedding should take place when the Moon is full, thus ensuring a long and happy marriage.

The Moon lunation takes around twenty-nine and a half days, starting from a full Moon and it continues until the next full Moon. For centuries civilizations bowed to the power of the Moon, crops were planted according to the Moon's phases, there were many rituals celebrating the power of the Moon. The Moon is still recognized today as having particular powers that affects planting and growing, people's emotions, and the ocean tides's of the world. There is still intrigue regarding the Moon and it holds a certain fascination for most people.

The recurring cycle of the phases of the Moon has been observed and honored by mankind since our earliest ancestors first turned their eyes upward towards the night sky in wonder. The unending cycle of the Moon is one of the most fundamental and readily observable rhythms of the natural world. And in every phase, every moment, our lives are influenced by the great lady of the heavens. We flow with the currents of the Moon whether we are conscious of them or not, and we can either choose to ignore Her influences, or we can make a conscious choice to incorporate the rhythms of our lives with the rhythms of the Moon.

Our Moon wisdom will grow through our commitment to experiencing and understanding the energies of the great lady. And, as with all relationships in our lives, our connection to the Moon will be a deeply personal and endlessly growing interaction. Watch the comings and goings of the Moon just as those who came before us have always done.

Begin by taking the time to notice what phase the Moon is in and where She is in the sky at the time you have chosen to greet Her. You will find that over time you will begin to tune to Her changing rhythms, and as you continue observe and to honor Her cycles, you will find yourself aligning more closely to the lunar energies.

So, starting now, take time some time out of your busy day to greet Her. Look up into the sky and find Her face in the Heavens above. Remember, some days you will need to seek Her out during the light of day. Then, open your arms and your heart to Her and greet Her as you would greet a dear friend. Allow yourself to stir with connection to Her light and beauty. Speak words of greeting and gratitude to the lovely lady who guides us.

i
WEAVING MOONLIGHT
Getting Stated on the Journey

"There she weaves by night and day,
A magic web with colors gay."
— Tennyson

Nothing can put things into perspective quite like the night sky. It has a way of making me feel I am part of the entire universe, with the Moon drawing me in. There is something comforting about her distant but nurturing presence. Like a guardian, the Moon has always been steadfastly at my back. I might have grown up to be an astronomer if I could have devoted myself entirely to the Moon. Unlike the Sun, I can gaze into the Moon endlessly, for she is never feels blinding. In fact, quite the opposite. The tarot teaches us that the Moon is about introspection. About reflecting back at ourselves the life we want to be living. When the sun jumps in feat first, it is the Moon who slowly moves into discernment.

Weaving Moonlight introduces seekers to a Moon cosmology, that saturates the heart and offers insights into the architecture of the universe, through myth, manifesting and magic. This isn't a new phenomenon, the idea that the Moon is a living organism with a soul and spirit. Native cultures have long lived in the lap of Moonlight. As we have seen, and will continue to explore, the Moon has been a beacon, a kind of indigenous Grandmother to many. Because of the way the Moon functions, developing practices around release and renewal is natural. In many ways provides a template organically to nurturing the soul. However applying Moon cosmology to our daily lives in clear and accessible ways can be challenging. The modern world doesn't naturally invite us to stop and dance under the Moon.

That is why I wrote this book. There is a modern theory that states within each part, the whole is reflected. To the seeker of wisdom and healing, the most important thing to realize is that you hold the key to knowing the Moonlight, weaving it into our lives, and knowing ourselves. The entirety of creation, of ourselves, becomes the voice of the infinite the Moonlight, the organic is an expression of the unity. When you accesses Weaving Moonlight, you are no longer separate from the rest of creation. Rather. I am the Moonlight, You are the Moonlight, All is the Moonlight.

Weaving Moonlight invites you to discover your most authentic self in contemplative and introspective practices to nurture the soul. The book is never ending, but rather a cycle that follows in rhythm with the Moon. The first part of the book, should take exactly 29 days to read, one full lunar cycle. I suggest reading along with each phase. Here you will explore the science and the lore of each Moon phase, and apply practice points, and intention building activities to unlock the power of specific phases. Each phase has several rituals and meditations. You need not to all of them, but rather return to them as you grow.

As we progress, Part two will explore the idea of the Moon as a divine representation of a triple Goddess archetype, as well as indigenous peoples understanding of the Moon's monthly faces. You will be invited to know holistic healing with the Moon, moreover come to understand how the elemental and planetary alignments of the Moon effect your life.

Along side all of this, is Lunar Journalling in alignment with the Moon to unlock your true nature. What the Moon reflects back to you is the key to manifesting the life you want. As you will come to discover, for millennia the Moon has always been a steadfast beacon. A constant reminder that every 29 days you can renew yourself, recommit to practice, and release any suffering in our lives.

TOOLS YOU WILL NEED

Many of the tools needed in this book are common household items. As you cultivate practices within the book you may feel called to acquire special crystals, essential oils, etc. However those things are simply an invitation to more, never an obligation for practice. The only tool you truly need is a journal. I get into more detail about your Lunar Journal in future chapters.

You may also want to set aside a specific small dark colored bowl. Like a dessert dish, or handleless Asian style teacup. Something small enough and unencumbered to hold with ease in your hands. This bowl will serve as a vessel for water and will often be used to reflect the Moon back to you in many of the manifesting activities. I use a small earthenware bowl, and dedicate it only for lunar activities.

Lastly, you will need an open heart. Many of the myths, meditations, and magic offered here may be new to you. They are designed to challenge and to inspire, cultivating your soul. Yet in no way are they "the law. The Love is the Law, a love that is stronger than fear. A love divine. Weave that love from the Moonlight and manifest the ultimate life.

Part I

waxing crescent

first quarter

waxing gibbous

full

waning gibbous

last quarter

waning crescent

lunar phases

i
THE NEW MOON
Days 1-3.5

*The new Moon of no importance
lingers behind as the yellow sun glares,
and is gone beyond the sea's edge
earth smokes blue;
the new Moon, in cool height above the bushes
brings a fresh fragrance of heaven to our senses.*
—D.H. Lawrence

And so we start, for the next 29 days the Moon's lunar cycle will lead and guide you. The New Moon is the birthing cycle of the Moon's various phases. We can recognize the New Moon in the sky as the first crescent we can see often following a period of darkness. This tiny sliver of Moon is your invitation to attract your heartfelt longings and focus on manifestation. The period of the New Moon is a good time to start new activities and to take action toward new ambitions, purposes, and directions. This is the time to plant, so that we may grow or create the pathway of your inner journey. Look deeply into your inner self, and by consciously moving your being into an alignment with the New and Full Moon cycle, you will find a potential to use the inner channels within your being. The challenge which confronts us at the New Moon cycle is one of self-expression through activity...primarily as one of us projecting ourselves out into the environment, society. This can include learning about what we hope to have manifested in our lives, the vision which we will choose to pursue, taking decisions to change unsatisfactory areas of our lives, and making new beginnings. The New Moon is a phase of renewal, and it is this energy that we can harness to aid our attempts to change.

STARTING A LUNAR JOURNAL

Writing about your experiences helps you understand yourself and see opportunities that may not have been apparent at first glance. Even if you don't think anything special has happened to you, trust me it has. The fundamental practice towards wellness and knowing is documentation. In your Lunar Journal you will write intentions, musings, aspirations. The goals you seek to manifest and the habits you wish to banish, all live in your Lunar Journal.

The Lunar Journal is your personal manifesto of experiences and truth. There is never a need to show it to anyone else, but by writing down your thoughts and then rereading them later, you will be able see the patterns of your soul. You'll see more clearly what you have learned about yourself, your feelings, your emotions, how you handle things--and you will likely also see what you have NOT learned yet. The things that cause us pain are often found to involve similar patterns of behavior, similar mistakes. In the process of thinking these things through, you may also discover a path toward healing.

I prefer handwriting in a book, over typing keys on a computer. Maybe I am old-fashioned, but more nuanced, the Lunar Journal is often more than just words. You might draw something from a dream, sketch out the set up to a ritual or even cut and past things that inspire you.

Many people think they can't journal, and so to start each lunar cycle has a series of questions as writing prompts. Feel free to adapt these questions for your own needs. Also dedicate some time to the activity, and don't rush. Journaling should feel like an invitation, not an obligation. I have found that when you take your time your inner self remains hidden. Just jot down what comes to your mind...words, phrases...sentences about how you relate to this phase of the Moon.

Lunar Journal: The New Moon

Take a few moments to sit with these questions. Allow your mind to release any expectations. Write the first thing that comes into your mind. Each night between now and the Full Moon return to your answers to these questions. How are they leading you towards rebirth?

- What is your inner self's new beginning?
- What seeds might you plant in your inner self so that you can grow, transform, or create yourself anew?
- How might you nourish your new beginning?
- What inspires your creativity?
- Is there a dream that you keep having? Do you think this dream has a lesson to teach you?

Planning For the New Moon

The New Moon is a perfect time to review your life, weighing the good and the bad. Celebrate all of your achievements moreover think about the things that you have wanted to do for many years, but have not yet been able to accomplish. What are these things? You still have time to do them. Choose the most important and consider what the first step towards fulfilling this goal would be. Write the steps down in your journal and vow to make it happen. What needs to be done to begin at the next New Moon?

Create a monthly ritual to be used when first viewing, greeting, and blessing the new Moon. Use some traditional folk elements such as plants and herbs, or use these as a basis for your creation. Compose and recite a short prayer, to the Moon that can be easily memorized for use at the beginning of each lunar month.

A Prayer to the New Moon

When reciting this prayer, light a white candle, focus your breathing and soften your gaze. Dedicate the merit of your intention to your highest self, to your rebirth into the life you want to be living and believe in the power of your words. When we believe we manifest.

Silver Moon nestling in the midnight sky,
Shine your ageless wisdom upon my soul.
Guide and nourish my spirits with your mysteries
So that I may flourish and grow under your beauty.

Oh lune of light, teach me the truths I so desire
And let me bathe in your silver aura.
Cleanse my body in your purifying light
And uplift my minds with your magic and majesty.

So shallI honor you with my hearts
And forever follow your illuminated path
To the centre of my souls.

When you have completed the manifestation, take a moment to reflect on how you might be feeling. Invite a deeper sense of wellness and well being into your heart and soul.

Understanding the New Moon

What is the ghostly image in the night sky? It's a new Moon. Its lighted half is facing entirely away from Earth. The image above is imaginary. It's as if you flew in a spaceship to a place where you could see the night side of the Moon. Why do we say imaginary? Because, when the Moon is new, its night face is facing us on Earth ... and we can't see the Moon at this time.

We can't see the new Moon from Earth, except during the stirring moments of a solar eclipse. Then the Moon passes in front of the sun, and the night portion of the Moon becomes visible to us, surrounded by the sun's fiery corona.

Once each month, the Moon comes all the way around in its orbit so that it is reasonably between us and the sun. If the Moon always passed directly between the sun and Earth at new Moon, a solar eclipse would take place every month. But that doesn't happen every month. Instead, in most months, the Moon passes above or below the sun as seen from our earthly vantage point.

Young Moon, visible a day or two after the new Moon phase. A young Moon is seen in the West after sunset. It's a Waxing crescent Moon. On the day of new Moon, the Moon rises when the sun rises. It sets when the sun sets. It crosses the sky with the sun during the day. That's why we can't see the new Moon in the sky. It is too close to the sun's glare to be visible. In addition its lighted hemisphere is facing away from us.

Then a day or two later, the Moon reappears, in the West after sunset. Then it's a slim Waxing crescent visible only briefly after sunset – what some call a young Moon. Each new lunar cycle is measured beginning at each new Moon. Astronomers call one lunar cycle a lunation.

Knowing the New Moon

This is the very beginning of the brand new lunar cycle, and that is the feeling it brings. Now is when we turn our attention to what is fresh and new, there is a feeling of excitement and apprehension. We are looking at a blank canvas, immersed in the possibilities of what may fill it. This is the time for vision, passion, and action. New ideas abound, inner desires surface, the vision is vivid, yet not quite defined. There is a bit of hesitation, as instinct warns that once the first step is made, the direction of the path is set. Yet the enthusiasm of the universe overcomes this hesitation, and we not only take the first step, but dive right in-impulsively, almost unknowingly.

New Moon is the phase of new beginnings. You may not be aware you are beginning anything at all, this is often a time with little conscious awareness of direction. This is a time of emotion, desire, and spontaneity. We are forming goals and intentions, not cohesive plans and rational ideas. We are in tune with ourselves, what we want and what we need; this self-knowledge is not filtered and subdued by the ' rational' facts, if, where, and how it fits into our plans. This is the phase of the visionary, we have a vision of where we are going, and a keen insight toward what is within.

Remember, all is new, the possibilities are endless. Ask yourself: "What do I want?" "What do I need?" "Where do I want to go?" Don't ask the hows and whys; shoulds and shouldn'ts. Not right now. This is a time to form your goal, your intent, and your vision. These things often happen spontaneously, on an almost subconscious level. Focus on it, and form a clear picture, develop awareness. Have a vision, a goal that is emotionally satisfying, and answers what your inner self is telling you?

We will form our intentions and act on them, whether deliberate or unknowingly. That's what this phase is about. It's not about the plans and details that go with goals. It has been said that a dream is a goal without a plan. Then this is the time to see, develop, and nurture the dream as it must come before the plan. We need trust and faith in ourselves, and our ability to manifest this dream. As the Lunar Cycle progresses, we will develop the plans, work out the details, acquire the resources, gather the information, adapting and evolving the vision we now hold as it becomes necessary. But first, the intention needs to be clear, you decide where you want to go, before looking at a map and planning the route or else the coarse of least resistance is liable to take you where you don't want to be.

There is a very common theme in everything relating to the New Moon Phase, which is very simply new. It's the beginning of the Lunar Cycle, the beginning of new goals and dreams, the beginning of a new level of self awareness. This is also the time for any other sort of new beginning. Start new projects, make positive changes, form new routines, get a new perspective on an old problem, or commit to a new and better attitude. This is a fresh start. Begin a new step or phase of a long-term project. Start reading a new book. Meet new people. Try a new recipe.

The cycle of life follows the Lunar Cycle. During this phase, she is not building and increasing, she is beginning. Although this is an appropriate and quite productive time for continued growth and building on what you've previously began, that's not the very most productive use of the energy. Following the Moon, mirroring her actions with your own you fall in perfect rhythm with the natural flow. The natural energy flow right now is taking what did not visibly exist and growing it into full, bright, beautiful manifestation.

The Moon is, or course, never gone or nonexistent. Lunar power and energy is extremely strong on the day of New Moon. It is power of darkness, what is unseen, what is before and between manifestations. By the end of this phase we can catch a brilliant shimmering glimpse of what is beginning to manifest into the visible world. This is the time to begin putting into action what has existed in your thoughts, ideas, emotions or soul that has not yet began to manifest into the visible world.

Are you looking for the perfect time to launch an important project or event? Although any phase during the Waxing portion of the lunar cycle is good for beginning things, the New Moon Phase adds it's own energy and force. With the entire cycle ahead, this phase is full of promise, enthusiasm and room for growth. This may be the perfect time for beginning things that need a lot of momentum, and have a long way to go. Things that are began during the New Moon have a tendency to perpetually evolve, sometimes lacking clear planning or structure. There is a vivid and inspirational quality, often attracting attention. This is a good time for endeavors of a creative, or spiritual nature, where perpetual and unforeseen evolution is a benefit. It's also a good time for things you want publicity, or public attention.

It is also well-suited (often better suited) for taking the next big step in an ongoing project. The lunar cycle is short, and most important undertakings span several cycles. The New Moon Phase is the beginning of the next cycle the end of the last cycle. It is something brand new, yet just another step in an ongoing spiral. When you find yourself at that point, of beginning something new that is a new beginning within an existing cycle, the New Moon phase May be the perfect time.

Moon Wish Manifesting

The New Moon is the birthing cycle of the Moon's various phases. Are you ready to attract your heartfelt longings by doing a Moon ritual focused on manifestation? The New Moon phase is an optimal time for planning and seeding your intentions. Seedlings need a period of gestation before they break through the soil and reach for the sunlight. This is also true for our cultivating our ideas and clearing the way for our visions to surface in reality. The New Moon, offers a nurturing environment where our intentions can establish roots before their miraculous manifestations begin to sprout and reach out to the stars.

SUPPLY SUGGESTIONS:
notebooks
pen and colored markers
scissors
scotch tape
candle
matches
incense
smudge sticks
meditation CDs

Prepare yourself a sacred space where your will perform the ceremony when the new Moon arrives.

Cleanse your sacred area with an opening prayer, a sage smudging, burning some incense. Light one or more candles.

Center your being and calm yourself in whatever way is appropriate for you. Take some deep cleansing breaths, slip in a meditation CD to listen to, and/or leisurely sip on a cup of relaxing herbal tea.

Open your notebook, and date the first page. Write down these words "I accept these things into my life now or something better for my highest good and for the highest good of all concerned." Or something similar. Below your affirmation statement, begin writing down your desires. Your list may consist of a single item or you may have several pages listing multiple items. Try not to limit yourself. If having many things in your life helps to fulfill you then don't deny yourself wanting these things.

During the month when an item on your new Moon list comes to you no not merely cross it off of your list. Take the time to rewrite the list in its entirety eliminating the manifested item from the listing. Revising your master list in this way is highly recommended. At the same time you may add whatever else that you have decided you would like. Feel free to reword any of the original phrases to better suit your life now. It is natural that your desires will change as time advances.

A second notebook will be used as a manifestation scrapbook where you can paste in pictures or catalog clippings of items that you are wanting to manifest. Creating manifesting scrapbooks or vision boards is a fun project to undertake, enjoy yourself! You will soon be amazed how these things begin to find their way into your life once you start this process.

Rededicating Your New Moon Intentions

Each month at the new Moon rededicate your intentions by renewing your list at a repeated ritual. This is accomplished by rewriting your list out using a fresh sheet of paper. Please don't get in the habit of simply scratching out the items you no longer desire and simply adding the new stuff to the bottom of your old list. You don't want clutter and sloppiness energies messing up the path meant to deliver new stuff into your life do you? Disregard any items that no longer feed your soul and add new things which will.

It is helpful to salt and pepper your manifest list with smaller items that will manifest quickly, such as tickets to the ballet, lunch with a friend, or a day at the spa. You may think that smaller things are too trivial to put on your intention list... Wrong! Things that tend to manifest with less effort still deserve to be written down. Write down everything that you desire, no matter how little or simple. If it is something that makes you happy, write it down.

Manifesting smaller items on our lists creates a steady flow of chi giving your list a boost. These smaller manifestations create movement, allowing an ebb and flow of the tides. We are dealing here with the Moon cycles after all. Besides, sometimes we forget to appreciate the smaller pleasures in our lives while we are waiting for the BIG stuff to come in. If you only write statements like, "I want to win the lottery" in your notebook then you are limiting yourself by not allowing abundance to flow to you from a multitude of avenues.

ii
Waxing Moon
Crescent • Days 3.5-6
First Quarter • Days 6-9.5
Gibbous Days • Days 10-13.5

Though the night was made for loving
And the day returns too soon
Yet we'll go no more a-roving
By the light of the Moon
          —Byron

The Moon now begins her delicate journey to fullness, each night increasing until She forms a 'horned Moon', and as the Moon increases, shining ever more brightly on the earth, She symbolizes the eternal rhythm of growth to maturity. This is considered the ideal time for manifestations geared towards drawing things to you, for attraction, or rituals of increase. These three days are dedicated to Persephone, the initiator.

Initiation or the start of a spiritual journey can be

reinforced by connecting to the energy of the Waxing Moon, visualizing the seeds planted now germinating and growing a the light of the Moon increases. A ritual performed now can be strengthened and added to throughout this phase. Candles, oils, potions, and herbal preparations made during this time vibrate with the energy of increase, hope, rebirth, and gentle light.

Choose a quiet place to watch the Moon, either during the day as She is rising, or later in the evening as She sails through the night sky. Take some of your favorite incense and, in the evening, a candle to burn. Spend time relaxing and breathing in the Moon's energy.

Feel yourself connecting with Her--imagine your energy flowing to Her, then flowing from Her to you again, filling you with light. Feel your energy growing as She grows.

Waxing Moon Manifestation

Candle are wonderful tools for centering ourselves to invite the growing Moon. There are two basic phases of the Moon that can be harnessed for candle manifestation. The time when the Moon appears to be growing larger is the time to do Lunar Manifestation work about invocation, attraction and bringing in; for example, attracting a lover or bringing in more abundance.

It is best to light your candle toward the early part of the Moon phase and completely burn it before the phase of the Moon completes.

SACRED SPACE PREPARATION

Prepare an area for sacred space in your home on a small table or nightstand. Using water and a paper towel, wipe down the area of your table that you intend to use as an altar in a counterclockwise motion, with the energy and intent that you are clearing space for your Lunar work. Arrange your candle in a votive candle holder, jelly jar, or cup (anything that will contain the wax as it melts), along with anything

else that represents the work that you are going to do on the altar in a way that is pleasing to you.

CANDLE PREPARATION

Unwrap the candle (be sure to remove the plastic wrapper too) and sit with the candle in your hands and meditate on your intent. Take a pencil, knife or some sharp object and carve words representing this work into the sides of the candle.

Anoint your candle with an appropriate oil, stroking it in a downward motion for clearing or an upward motion for attracting. After anointing your candle, you are ready for the Lunar Manifestation.

RAISING ENERGY & SETTING THE MANIFESTATION

Place your candle in the holder. Light incense that is pleasing to you and use it to clear the energies surrounding you and your altar space.

Raise your energy through dance, chanting, singing, visualization gets your vibration up high. When you feel you are at a peak, light your candle and speak your manifestation words.

Once you have taken several moments to appreciate your work, ground your raised energy by imagining it returning to

Mother Earth through your feet (and your hands, if you want) on the floor. Eating something will also bring you back down to a grounded level.

Candle Maintenance

Your candle will need to be put out when you leave your house or go to sleep, but the effectiveness will remain if you snuff your candle instead of blowing it out. When you need to snuff your candle, use a shot glass, cup, dish, candle snuffer or pinch out the candle with moist fingers. Say, "I thank you, powers of earth, water, fire and air" When you relight your candle, repeat the key message from your manifestation in a few words or a sentence.

Completion

When your candle has completely burned down (ideally, before the end of the Moon cycle) take any remaining wax out of the holder. This wax may be given back to Mother Nature by burying in the ground. For an invoking/bringing in candle, bury it on your property or close to your home; for a clearing/banishing candle, bury it somewhere away from your home or leave it in a crossroads. Your manifestation work is complete, your work now is to envision, expect and receive the positive results.

Lunar Journal
Waxing Moon

Take a moment to reflect in your Lunar Journal, what has been inspiring? What keeps coming up for you? Maybe it is attracting a new love, or committing to meditation to soothe the mind? The Waxing Moon is the time to step into the act of naming your intention. Here are some examples of intentions.

- Creating abundance
- Inviting success
- Attracting a soulmate into your life

Take a moment to reflect writing on a piece of paper what you hope to achieve. Now is the time to create your first ritual around the Waxing Moon.

Discovering the Waxing Crescent

A Waxing crescent Moon – sometimes called a young Moon – is always seen in the west after sunset. At this Moon phase, the Earth, Moon and sun are located nearly on a line in space. If they were more precisely on a line, as they are at new Moon, we wouldn't see the Moon. The Moon would travel across the sky during the day, lost in the sun's glare.

A Waxing crescent Moon is far enough away from that Earth-sun line to be visible near the sun's glare – that is, in the west after sunset. This Moon phase is seen one day to several days after new Moon. On these days, the Moon rises one hour to several hours behind the sun and follows the sun across the sky during the day. When the sun sets, and the sky darkens, the Moon pops into view in the western sky.

Note that a crescent Moon has nothing to do with Earth's shadow on the Moon. The only time Earth's shadow can fall on the Moon is at full Moon, during a lunar eclipse. There is a shadow on a crescent Moon, but it's the Moon's own shadow. Night on the Moon happens on the part of the Moon submerged in the Moon's own shadow. Likewise, night on Earth happens on the part of Earth submerged in Earth's own shadow.

Because the Waxing crescent Moon is nearly on a line with the Earth and sun, its illuminated hemisphere – or day side – is facing mostly away from us. We see only a slender fraction of the day side: a crescent Moon. Each evening, because the Moon is moving eastward in orbit around Earth, the Moon appears farther from the sunset glare. It is moving farther from the Earth-sun line in space. Each evening, as the Moon's orbital motion carries it away from the Earth-sun line, we see more of the Moon's day side. Thus the crescent in the West after sunset appears to wax, or grow fatter each evening.

You sometimes see a pale glow on the darkened portion (night side) of a crescent Moon. This glow is due to light reflected from Earth's day side. It's called earthshine.

Knowing the Waxing Crescent

The Waxing Moon is now visible and increasing in size and brightness as she goes from a sliver to a crescent. The first, thin glimpses we may have seen in the New Moon Phase are taking shape, becoming a solid form. This is the energy we feel during this phase, the beginnings of solidity. Our visions and intentions are becoming goals and plans. Momentum is building, we are beginning to see and feel the formation of what we have began. Visions are beginning to evolve into manifestation.

Awareness is Waxing with the Moon. We are moving from what to how. Our vision is clear, and direction is chosen. Now we must find a path that will lead us in this direction. This is a time of seeking, and developing. We are gathering information, turning our ideas into plans. We are becoming aware of what tools and resources are needed. We are encountering details, confronting the challenges we must face. The vision held on New Moon is going from a dream to a goal; from an idea to a plan. We are becoming aware of how the vision must evolve, sorting out the possible from the impossible, gathering the resources and strength to follow a path that is possible, yet maintains the intent formed in our minds, hearts, and souls.

Don't lose sight of the vision developed in the New Moon Phase. During the Crescent Moon Phase we encounter the reality of what it will take to make it happen. This can be stressful, even daunting. This is where we become aware of the effort required to bring a vision into manifestation. Ask yourself why you chose this goal, why was it so important? Feed your inner fire, reminding yourself of the desires and needs that your goals and visions fulfill.

The Moon in the sky has moved from darkness or a glimmer of light in the New Moon Phase to a slender, but solid easily visible crescent during this phase. Likewise, intangible ideas and inspirations are taking solid, tangible form. This means complications, commitments, and sometimes second thoughts. This is the time to actively push forward, and make a conscious effort to maintain and build momentum. Inner doubts, skeptical people, and little glitches offer you a way out. It may be easy to give up on your new ideas and goals and there will surely be something convenient to blame. This is the phase when you are challenged to draw on your inner strength, stand up to criticism, trust yourself, and - above all - make an effort.

The Moon is now a visible, solid form in the sky. However, she is only visible for a brief while, and her slim crescent appears almost fragile in the vast darkness of nightfall. To the observer, with no knowledge of astronomy or the cycles it would seem as if her progress was fleeting. Yet it steadily increases, each night a little bigger, visible for a little longer. As our lives follow the path of the Moon, we find ourselves facing solid progress and promise of growth, but it seems to be fragile and fleeting we wonder if our feeble efforts can hold up to the vast darkness we need to shine through.

Don't procrastinate, and don't back down. That is the best way to ensure the survival of your new plans and projects, or the progress of existing ones. This is a busy time, but not with as much fun and enthusiasm as New Moon. This is a time to get serious and dig in. This is when you get ahead, or get behind. It's still a good time for beginning things, and with more practical and detail oriented energy, it's an even better time than New Moon for forming good habits. On the other hand, it may be easy to fall into bad habits, so be careful. It's also a good time for gathering and analyzing resources. For example, money, skills, and time are important resources in many projects; this is a good time for budgeting, beginning school/training , or scheduling.

Pay attention to stress management during this phase. It's going to be a busy time, there's a lot to do, details to deal with, little glitches and challenges developing... This isn't the time to give up, let things slide, and let your work pile up. It also isn't a good idea to knock yourself out trying to do everything, especially all at once. Rest, relax, and take a deep breath when you need to. Don't slip into workaholic mode and use up your inner resources; just don't slip into inertia and apathy either. The most important thing right now is to develop, and maintain confidence and determination.

Discovering the Lunar First Quarter

The Crescent Moon Phase is just as good as the New Moon Phase for beginning big projects. It will bring less inspiration, but more grounding to your ventures. Things began during the Crescent Phase tend to have a progressive, even revolutionary quality. There is some sort of resistance, but facing the resistance produces meaningful progress. There is a quality of releasing the past. This is an excellent time to begin progressive endeavors or things aimed at change. For example, this would be a particularly good time for beginning a social or political movement; starting an innovative technology business; beginning a different lifestyle. Despite the ingrained tendency toward facing resistance, things began now tend to progress and grow more rapidly than things began during New Moon.

In ongoing projects and situations, Crescent Moon is the time to begin pulling things together, or take small steps. Where you have been scattering your forces, or things have gotten off course, use this time this time to put them back on track. It's a good time to begin a new phase of a long-term plan.

Remember, this is the first visual manifestation of the new Lunar Cycle. Use this time for things that are approaching the manifestation stage. It's also a perfect time for building on and expanding what you have began previously. As the Moon is becoming a visible, solid form in the night sky is the time to solidify scattered or undefined plans and ideas into action

A first quarter Moon shows half of its lighted hemisphere half of its day side to Earth.
But we officially call this Moon a quarter and not a half because it is one quarter of the way around in its

orbit of Earth, as measured from one new Moon to the next.

This Moon appears half-lit to us, and half Moon is a beloved name (although not an official one). Still, it's good to recall that the illuminated portion of a first quarter Moon truly is just a quarter. On the night of first quarter Moon, we see half the Moon's day side, or a true quarter of the Moon. Another lighted quarter of the Moon shines just as brightly in the direction opposite Earth!

A first quarter Moon rises at noon and is high overhead at sunset. It sets around midnight.

First quarter Moon comes a week after new Moon. Now, as seen from above, the Moon in its orbit around Earth is at right angles to a line between the Earth and sun. As the Moon orbits Earth, it changes phase in an orderly way. Follow these links to understand the various phases of the Moon.

Knowing the Lunar First Quarter

The Lunar First Quarter is time when the Moon is mid-way between the Waxing Crescent and the Full Moon. The deceptive imagery of fragility and hesitancy in the Waxing Moon are long gone. She is brilliantly lit, growing rapidly, and visible not only a good portion of the night, but in day as well. Strong and prominent, she victoriously casts her light, and casts her manifestation of confidence and success. Yet she has not reached Full Moon, we are only half way through the Waxing cycle. She has achieved brilliant light, high visibility, and solid form, but far from reaching the goal. She has simply passed the milestone of uncertainty; strength and momentum abound.

Our visions and inspirations, mere vague yet exciting notions at New Moon have taken shape, and gained momentum along with the Moon. Plans are becoming solid and real, our inner visions are coming to the attention of others. Excitement and enthusiasm are returning and things are happening, the vision is manifesting. We are shining brightly now, but, like the Moon, we still have a long way to go. Past the details and glitches of the Crescent Phase, we may be facing more real challenges. However these challenges have a way of exciting and stimulating, because we are also beginning to see some real effects of our efforts; there is something solid to fight for.

The First Quarter Phase is often referred to as 'crisis of action' because now is the time to move forward. The vision was born during New Moon, it faced the stresses of development during Crescent Moon, and now it's ready to be put into action. Move forward, build momentum, and take action. The question is how? We've defined our goal, and developed our resources. Now we need to refine the plan and act on it. We are beginning to see progress, take it and run with it. But don't run blindly, things are propelled forward with great momentum, and the key is to know where you're going, and how you'll get there, so you can make the most of this momentum.

There is a feeling of success, and a sense of accomplishment in the air. Yet the goal has not yet been reached, success has not been achieved. Many people will feel a surge in confidence (or ego) during the First Quarter Phase. It's all to easy to think things are going well, you are working hard, the goal is within reach. However, if you don't pay attention, and make sure all is going well, and that you are working hard in the right direction, that goal which felt so close could slip away before you even realize it. This is a time it's important to be sure of yourself (not only your actions) deep down. Confident and successful feelings based on the beginnings of accomplishments can be great. But they can be fragile. On some level we know it's premature to think we've won the battle before it's over. But things are progressing so fast we feel it anyway-until someone or something points out how far we still have to go. That's why it's important to be aware of how far we've come, and how far we have left. Be realistic, make a plan, tell yourself you can do it – and do it. Don't set yourself up for a fall.

The Moon is in solid form, and shining brightly. The energy level is high; so is the level of activity. The First Quarter Moon Phase is what we make of it. In the Crescent Phase, we encountered problems to be solved and things to be done. In this phase we take deliberate action. This is an excellent time for planning, structuring, making decisions and striving for efficiency and productivity. It's usually easier to develop confidence during First Quarter, so if you have confidence and self esteem issues, actively work on them. This also makes it a good time for taking on difficult or challenging projects. This is a good time to begin a health or exercise program, organize, remodel, change routines, whatever will get things on track and moving in the right direction.

Take a decisive and assertive approach. This isn't the time to 'decide not to decide.' Things are happening, probably faster than you realize, and you want to shape the way they develop. Push for progress, and be quick to take action. There is a lot of energy and forward momentum, tap into it and get things done. Remember, that others are feeling the same lunar energy you are. There is an active, confident, and assertive quality to the mood of most people. It's probably best to avoid conflicts, when possible, unless you want a confrontation. When you find yourself at odds with others, try for compromise, but remember the saying, "If you act like a doormat, people will walk all over you." This is truer now than during any other lunar phase. Independence and individuality are important elements during this phase. Do your own thing, and do it well? Don't interfere in the progress of others, but don't let them interfere in yours either.

Lunar Journal:
First Quarter Uniqueness

What makes you unique? Sets you apart from the crowd? Take the time during the First Quarter to write in your journal the qualities you love about yourself, and what you hope to release.

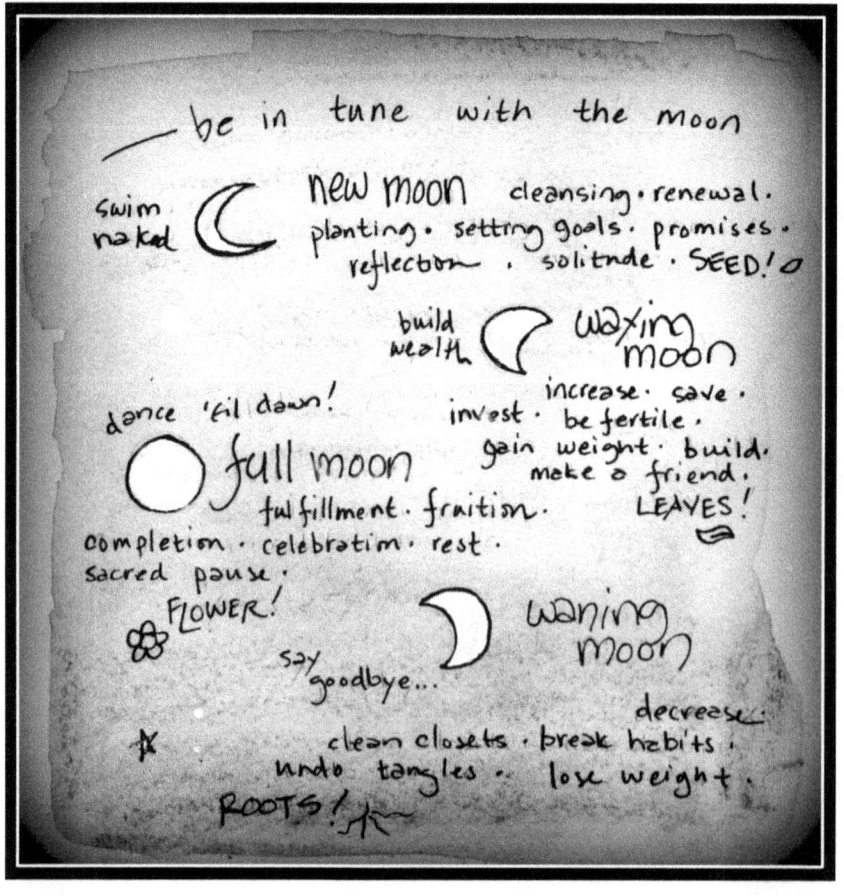

Discovering The Waxing Gibbous Moon

The Waxing gibbous Moon appears high in the East at sunset. It's more than half-lighted, but less than full. This Moon phase comes between one and two weeks after new Moon.

The Moon has moved in its orbit so that it's now relatively far from the sun in our sky. A Waxing gibbous Moon rises during the hours between noon and sunset. It sets in the wee hours after midnight. People sometimes see a Waxing gibbous Moon in the afternoon, shortly after Moonrise, while it's ascending in the East as the sun is descending in the West. It's easy to see a Waxing gibbous Moon in the daytime because, at this phase of the Moon, a large fraction of the Moon's day side is facing our way. Thus a Waxing gibbous Moon is more noticeable in the sky than a crescent Moon, with only a slim fraction of the lunar day side visible. Also, a Waxing gibbous Moon is far from the sun on the sky's dome, so the sun's glare isn't hiding it from view.

Any Moon that appears more than half lighted but less than full is called a gibbous Moon. The word gibbous comes from a root word that means humpbacked. You can see the humpbacked shape of the Waxing gibbous Moon.

Knowing the Waxing Gibbous Moon

The Moon is so nearly full, you may have to look twice, or even consult an astrological calendar as we approach the end of the Gibbous Phase. She is brilliant, nearly round, illuminating the darkness of night. Truly a breathtaking sight. Her energy is so strong you can feel it as you gaze at the silvery disc overhead. She is nearly full. Nearly, but not quite. It almost seems as if she is poised, yet hesitating, taking a deep breath before her big night. With time and patience, she proceed along her path. It will come. It will be soon.

If we bring our lives into rhythm with the natural cycles, we find ourselves following the path of the Moon. We are poised and ready, the goal is so near we can almost touch it, almost reach it. Almost, yet something is stopping us. We just don't feel prepared, or it isn't exactly coming together as it should. There is one more detail, or one missing element. We encounter a last minute glitch. Something isn't quite right, something isn't quite ready. So very close, but not quite, not yet. Do we give up, after working this long and hard, after pouring so much energy into it in the First Quarter Phase? Not if we are following the Moon's path; not if we are following her example and flowing with her energy. We continue, certain that it will happen, it will come, and it will be soon.

Look at the Moon, and feel the Moon. Draw from, join in her strength and certainty. The Gibbous Phase holds a great deal of power and potential. It may take some patience and determination to tap into it. We find ourselves at the precarious point of being very close to a goal. The vision born at New Moon is nearly materialized. We may think we've made it. Then something comes up, but don't look at it as a bad thing. This phase is about refining, fine-tuning, and tuning in. What you have begun may seem ready, but it can be better. Challenges, really, are always opportunities in disguise. But this is more true than ever during the Gibbous Phase. When you find yourself encountering glitches in your plans, realize tat it is fortunate they were discovered at this stage, and most likely the result will be improving and enriching your endeavors.

Impatience is so strong you can feel it in the air during Gibbous Phase. Yet patience is one of your best allies. However, this isn't the sit quietly and wait type patience. This phase call for having the patience to do things right, analyze, refine, strengthen, perfect There is far too much to do for idly waiting, or for rushing it too fast. Be careful, be certain, take criticism as constructive (even if it's not intended that way). Just watch the Moon, taking her time, developing the perfect form to create a spectacular display when the moment has come, and not before. Follow her lead, and as always, you won't go wrong.

The vision was born at New Moon. It has developed, strengthened through the phases and made great leaps forward during First Quarter Moon. Now it is on the brink of manifestation. If there was ever a bad time to give up, this is it! Work on solidifying your plans, and double check everything. Take advantage of the analytical and refining tendencies of this phase for anything that you need to revise. This is a good time for any kind of precision work, or reviewing and fine-tuning.

The Gibbous Phase is a good time for reviving what has been let slide. If you have (good) habits and routines you've strayed from, this is the time to work on getting them back. Skills and knowledge can get foggy too. If you have things you've learned, but haven't studied in a while, or skills you haven't practiced in some time, use this phase to 'brush-up'. You will find it comes back more easily than you think. This can also be a good time for developing natural talents. If you have flair for art (as an example), but have never tried to fine-tune your skills, this is a good time for it.

Though we have nearly reached Full Moon, the light is still increasing, we are still in the Waxing, growing portion of the cycle. It is still an appropriate time to start a project, or launch something new. Unless you want to encounter the resistance of trying to promote growth in something with ingrained diminishing tendencies, this is your last chance (or wait a couple weeks before the next cycle). Therefore, most often, the kinds of things we begin during this phase ore those we have been procrastinating on, rather than things that were planned and targeted for launching in this phase. If you don't want new beginnings during Waning Moon, and haven't got around to starting it yet, it's now or never. Not really never, but you'll have to wait a couple of weeks.

We have a tendency (it's human nature) to easily avoid and procrastinate, but if we're running out of time we suddenly become ready and impatient. You can call it synchronicity; you didn't plan it this way, yet this kind of energy fits well with the gibbous phase. As Full Moon is so very near, there is a feeling of impatience in the air. As so many things are almost complete, but not quite ready, there is a natural "mad rush' of sorts. So if you find yourself frantically scrambling to launch something that you hadn't got around to, yet suddenly can't wait for, don't feel that you've gotten out of tune. However, do inject some logic before you get carried away. Ask yourself a few questions. Can it wait until the next cycle? If so, are you actually ready; how much could it benefit from more preparation time?

Like the other phases the Gibbous Phase will bring it's own, unique energy and inclination to thing began now (whether this is when you planned the launch, or it was a last minute impulse). Things began during the Gibbous Phase are likely to need refining, and fine-tuning. There is a tendency to perpetually seek improvement. This is a good time for launching things that are really a rough idea, the refining, perfecting, and tweaking will come quite naturally. It's also a good time for beginning generally analytical, or highly detail oriented projects.

Prosperity Manifestation

SUPPLIES:
Silver coin
Cauldron or pot

Half fill the pot with water and drop a silver coin into it. Position the pot or cauldron so the light of the Full Moon shines onto the water. Gently sweep your hands above the surface, symbolically gathering up the Moon's silver.

While you are gathering the Moon's silver, say:
"La Luna, beautiful Lady of the Moon, bring to me your wealth right soon. Fill my hands with silver and gold. All you give, my hands can hold."

Repeat this chant three times. When you are finished, pour the water upon the Earth.

The Full Moon
Days 13.75- 17.5

*The Moon is a loyal companion.
It never leaves. It's always there, watching, steadfast, knowing us in our light and dark moments, changing forever just as we do. The Moon understands what it means to be human. Uncertain. Alone.
Cratered by imperfections.*

— Tahereh Mafi

Full Moon evenings are a time for rejuvenation, a time to connect with your vision and refine your intention. At the time of the Full Moon there is a greater opportunity to overcome obstacles in one's nature, and let go. The Full Moon is the point at which we can see an entire side of the moon, and is the most powerful phase. This is when the Moon is seen in glorious fullness, and we welcome enlightenment and heightened psychic awareness. This is the time when everything comes together; a time of ideas, but also a time of commitment.

Every month, the Full Moon reveals herself with different meanings, which we will discover in chapters to come. Know that all Full Moons are invitations to manifest change. You may have noticed in you life that there is a vibration shift when the moon is Full. Many see this shift most in our sleeping. Often the Full Moon brings an insomnia, and of course the misconception that the moon causes lunacy.

What is true is the moon changes our internal tide, much as she impacts the oceans' gravitational pull. The Full Moon has a power that can support us in the most wonderful ways if we allow ourselves to attune to it. One of the simplest ways to attune to lunar energy is to bask considering the moon during the days of fullness. This simple practice will help shift your inner rhythms in a natural way. This is also a time to be generous with yourself and allow more time for creative pursuits.

Full Moon energies are highly sensual so this is a time to allow yourself to enjoy the sensual pleasures of life. Your may find your digestion is stronger at this time of month it is the ideal time for a lavish dinner party with friends and family. Make your favorite meals, decorate your home, and toast each other with your favorite drinks while you relish in the sensual delights of good company, fine food, and the tastes and smells of the season. If you are in an intimate relationship you may notice that your senses are heightened at this time of month in a way that offers new layers of delight to your lovemaking. Full Moon nights are the perfect time to stay up long past bedtime savoring your loved one and celebrating the closeness that you share.

Full Moon Love Manifestations

Full Moon love manifestations have to be timed more specifically than most other witchcraft manifestations, though you have about a 4 day window to really capture the full Moon's unique energy. Approximately 2 days before the actual full Moon moment, and then 2 days afterwards. Even so, you should try to perform your manifestation as close to the true full Moon as possible.

Harness that full Moon power with this love manifestation. This is also a potent fire manifestation so you will need somewhere that you can safely light a fire. Outdoors is best but a fireplace, wood stove or even a cast-iron cauldron would do. Other than that, you will need to have:

SUPPLIES
A handful or two of coarse salt
Dried red rose petals
A place to burn a fire safely

This manifestation takes 3 nights, starting the night before the official full Moon date. Get a small fire going (you can use any type of wood for that). Stand before the fire toss in some salt, and say,

Let his heart burn for me,
Sparked under the light of the Moon,
Let his heart burn for me,
Bring him to me soon.

Obviously, change the text from "his" to "her" if needed. Toss in some of the rose petals, and repeat again. Let the flames burn for a few more minutes if you wish or extinguish the fire. Do the same ritual for the next 2 nights.

A new love or loving opportunity should come into your life before the next Full Moon. Once you have completed this manifestation, let the Moon take over and release yourself from any thoughts or expectations. Just know that the Moon is on your side!

The Full Moon is also an opportune time of the month for purging rituals to take place. The light the full moon offers illuminates those things that are interfering with our lunar alignment. Once we have become enlightened to ways that are blocking us, the easier to let go. The full moon ritual is for releasing or purging the things in our lives that no longer serve us such as addictions to food, drugs, or sex, relinquishing suffering involved in hurtful relationships, discharging physical and emotional pains, etc.

Lunar Journal: Full Moon Crossroads

We now find ourselves at a crossroads, what are we harnessing and what are we letting go? What is the perfectly imperfect contentment we seek? As yourself these questions under the full moon light,

- What is your most indispensable possession and why?

- What makes you feel safe?

- Once, when your feelings were hurt, what happened?

- Describe a time when you felt vengeful, what was it like, and how did you move past it?

We will use these entries in our next activity, Full moon Purging.

Full Moon Purging

Write down on separate slips of paper the things you want to release or change and using.

Make a small fire, either with a fire prof dish or using a candle. Cleanse your sacred area with an opening prayer, a sage smudging, and/or by burning some incense. Invite your guides, angels, masters, or teachers to be at your side throughout the ceremony.

Light one or more candles. Look to the skies. Breathe in the night air.

One by one, read out loud the words you have written on each slip of paper. Set your intention to release the item (or addiction or attitude) from your life. Set it to fire and place it in the caldron. If you have a campsite barbecue or bonfire going that's l, just toss the slips of paper into the fire one by one. If you are doing this ritual with a group of others take turns reading your words. If these things are too personal to read out loud, read them silently to yourself.

Remember, our words have power. Saying - "Be Gone" audibly and loudly can be very freeing.

Go ahead, howl at the moon if you've a mind to. Have some fun! Thank the spirits. Be safe.
Put out the fire.

Discovering the Full Moon

At full Moon, we are seeing all the Moon's day side. And that's what makes a full Moon look full. At full Moon, the Moon and sun are on a line, with Earth in between. It's as though Earth is the fulcrum of a seesaw, and the Moon and sun are sitting on either end of the seesaw. So as the sun sets in the West, the full Moon rises. When the sun is below our feet at midnight, the full Moon is highest in the sky. When the sun rises again at dawn, the full Moon is setting.

If there is a lunar eclipse, it must happen at full Moon. It's only at the full Moon phase that Earth's shadow, extending opposite the sun, can fall on the Moon's face.

In many ways, a full Moon is the opposite of a Dark Moon. At both the dark and full phases, the Moon is on a line with the Earth and sun. At new Moon, the Moon is in the middle position along the line. At full Moon, Earth is in the middle. Full Moon always comes about two weeks after new Moon, when the Moon is midway around in its orbit of Earth, as measured from one new Moon to the next.

Knowing the Full Moon

Half the Lunar cycle has been spent striving for this point. The Full Moon, in all her splendid glory shines brilliantly in the night sky, the earth glows with her divine silver light. The shadows seem vibrant and alive. It is a breathtaking sight, enlightening and mysterious. The darkness of night is illuminated, yet there is much we sense and cannot see. The light of the Moon, along with her power, has reached a peak. We see it, we feel it. The level of energy is higher on Full Moon than any other time of the month.

The Sun illuminates the Moon; she transforms and reflects his light upon the Earth. The illuminated Earth transforms and reflects her light, producing a mystical, silvery glow. These energies of illumination and reflection are ingrained into the phase of Full Moon. We reflect upon our lives and selves, we see more deeply into our own souls, as well as others. We are drawn to the illusive and mysterious.

The power of the Moon is unmistakable, tangible. We see it, feel it, and sense it. We feel our own power, and the power of the world around us. The Moon is the natural astrological ruler of emotions. When she is riding high, so are our emotions. We aren't happy, we're elated; we aren't mad, we're furious; we aren't interested, we're excited; we aren't sad, we're depressed.

This is a powerful time, of excess and extremes, which can manifest in a positive or negative way.

Full Moon is one of the most powerful and influential times in the natural cycle, and probably the most widely accepted (even by many skeptics) proof of astrological influence on our lives. Everyone has seen and felt the effects, first hand. There is an out-of-control tendency that can make it difficult to harness this energy. The first step is awareness. Don't enter this phase unaware of and out of touch with your emotions, or you likely won't know what to do when the emotional high-tide comes. Make sure you have used the Waxing phases to learn, grow, build and structure. If you approach Full Moon feeling like your life is spinning out of control, it just might.

Although we are only half way through the entire Lunar Cycle, there is a feeling of culmination. A goal has been reached. The building, evolving, Waxing light of the past couple of weeks has manifested. And what a spectacular manifestation it is! You will find things you have worked on, and built coming together at this time. Remember the vague visions of New Moon? Now illuminated, we can see them clearly. If they have survived, and you have put the effort into them, they are now a manifestation. Realistically, few goals are reached or projects completed in a couple of weeks time. However, there is a sense of completion and manifestation in some form. Perhaps the idea is just becoming a solid plan, or one phase of a project is completed. Whatever the case, even if it seems to be only in your own perspective, things are more real and solid. Something has been achieved. If you have been going in the wrong directions, you will see the results of that be manifested into solid form as well. Preparation and the right mind frame are key in successful, productive use of this notorious Moon Phase.

The Moon has reached her peak; from the moment of Full Moon the light will begin decreasing. The period of growth and time for beginnings is past. This is the most active period of change. This time can be useful for changing or breaking habits and routines. Bring things to an end, where needed. This is also a highly creative time, with endless poems, songs, and works of art using Full Moon as a subject, demonstrating the point. Make use of the creative influence for artistic endeavors, or creative thinking. Just be careful of coming to firm decisions fight now (especially on the day of Full Moon), as logic isn't necessarily a strong point right now.

There are many dark corners in our lives, and ourselves, both small and large scale. In 'dark corners' I don't necessarily mean negative things, these are (at least partially) hidden or unnoticed things. With Full Moon, comes light, allowing us to see in those normally invisible, dark corners, just as the brilliant Moonlight allows us to see in the normally dark night. Use this time to take a closer look at things, see hidden potential, look for mistakes, and find opportunities. You can also get a clear insight into yourself, as your emotions are much stronger than usual.

As energy and emotions run high, arguments and conflicts are more likely at Full Moon. Although often difficult, compromise is important. In astrological terms, this is an opposition; the Sun is in the opposite position of the Moon. We often find ourselves completely at odds with someone else. It's important to remember, that this can be quite valuable, useful or informative. Opposite can manifest in different ways. When you look in a mirror, the image you see reflected is opposite the actual image, yet reflects it accurately. When you encounter opposition, ask yourself if, in some way, it reflects aspects of yourself or your situations you have not been seeing. Other times, these conflicts can provide valuable insight or information. True, absolute opposites each have elements the other is missing. When you encounter opposition ask yourself if this person or event is giving you information and understanding that you have overlooked, and could make your approach complete and balanced.

It is no longer a good time for beginnings, the flow of energy is shifting. Full Moon is the balance point, or imbalance as it may be, in between Waxing and Waning. She is neither growing nor shrinking, she is full 100% illuminated. For an instant, a fleeting moment, there is total fulfillment, completion, achievement, and illumination. After that moment, the light is Waning, slowly and gradually. This phase carries the energy of the moment of Full Moon, as well as the first gradual steps into the Waning portion of the cycle. This is a good time for completing long-term projects, or completing a phase of them.

This can be a good time for public displays, drawing attention, or presentations. There is a high energy, and highly emotional quality to Full Moon, so don't draw attention to potentially controversial things, unless you want a controversy. This is a time for putting on a show, and getting a dramatic response.

The other, quite obvious factor in the influences this phase brings is, of course, light. It's a good time for evaluation, as things are illuminated figuratively, as well as literally. As we enter the Waning phase, there is necessary decreasing and endings. Take a good look at your important projects and plans. Where are you stretching yourself, or your resources too thin? This is the time to begin 'weeding out' the unnecessary. There is a focus on excesses right now, and if you can step back and be objective (so that you aren't inclined to go to excesses) it is a good time for spotting excesses.

Full Moon Meditation

This meditation is for giving thanks for abundance and fruition and for the honoring and release of what has been completed in your life, and work that requires the intense energies of the Moon in her fullest state. Some examples of the later would be cleansing your crystals, making Moon alchemy water or even creating an Epsom salt detox bath.

Get creative during this time but make sure to take time for yourself to let go, detox and release. Anoint your sacred space with smudge sage and light a white candle. Below are instruction on how I proceed to cleanse and activate my chakras through Full Moon Meditation.

If possible find an area to stand or sit barefoot upon the earth.

Close your eyes or keep them softly focused and feel the Moon beams bathing you in cleansing and purifying energy.

If you are in the sunlight then go into your bed room make a clean and comfortable spot imagining the Moon beams and soothing properties of the Moon light. You can also charge a bath with Epsom salts and calming herbs like sage and lavender.

Breathe deeply. Feeling your lungs and diaphragm expand to it's maximum capacity. Pause for a few seconds and slowly exhale imagining the diaphragm as "up flying" or pulling the diaphragm (your belly button) towards the spine.

Imagine your inhale and exhale creating a figure eight or infinity symbol.

Imagine all areas of the body releasing tension starting from the feet going all the way up to the muscle of the face. Let go of all muscle tension. Surrender.

Inhale, imagine roots from the legs or the base of the spine diving down into the earth.

Guide this energy up towards the very top of the head or the crown. Imagine a white lotus flower on the very top of your head and through this blossoming lotus flower white glowing pure light is pouring into your body.

Covering like a blanket of snow all of the body seeping into each pore. Cleansing your inner being.

Feel comfortable bliss. Now dive down in the earth as exhale. Letting go of anything that no longer serves you. Anxiousness-Anger-Sadness.

Imagining the white light again drawing it from the earths core through you, up each energy center through your body *and penetrating into the universes and endless stars.*

Imagine bliss, peace and love showering again back down on the earth. That energy returning to you as cool, soft, angel white light wings surrounding you.

Placing your hands in prayer, lifting your hands to third eye center and bowing.

We end by letting our hands come back down to heart center.

Take a moment to ground and center, bringing your awareness back to your surroundings. Note in your Lunar Journal any thoughts, feelings, or new experiences.

Magic Moon Water

Leave a jug of spring water out in the light of the Full Moon. This water is excellent for washing your face to impart beauty and purity and can also be used to energetically cleanse crystals and imbue them with the magic of the Full Moon.

Full Moon Oil

13 drops of sandalwood essential oil
9 drops of vanilla essential oil or extract
3 drops of jasmine essential oil
1 drop of rose essential oil

Mix before a full Moon. Charge in a clear container or vial in the light of the full Moon. Use to anoint candles or yourself for full Moon rituals or just when you feel like you need the Moons energy.

Full Moon Heart's Desire

To ask for your heart's desire in a pure beeswax candle, carve or engrave what you wish to manifest into the candle wax. Light the candle, and with your eyes fixed upon the flame, concentrate on your heart's desire being granted by the Goddess Moon.

When this thought is firmly in your mind, whisper softly: "Luna, mother of all love and light, grant me my heart's desire (say exactly what you wish for). Grant my wishes, fulfill my heart's desire. Shine on me tonight."

Blow out the candle flame, but hold the image of it in your mind's eye for as long as possible. As you think of the candle's flame, know for sure that your wish has been heard. Within the space of one lunar cycle, your heart's desire should be granted.

iv
THE WANING MOON
Disseminating • Days 17.5-21
Last Quarter   Days 21-24.5
Waning Crescent • Days 24.5-27

And still thou wanest, pallid Moon!
The encroaching shadow grows apace;
Heaven's everlasting watchers soon
Shall see thee blotted from thy place.
—William Cullen Bryant

The Waning Moon favors completion, letting go, and finishing things off. It is not the time to begin new projects since the energy of this cycle is diminishing, and you will find yourself less apt to follow through when the new cycle begins. The new project that you are so anxious to start, is going to have to wait if you want it to be a success.

The Waning Moon is a time for "getting rid of" which means that any workings you do are going to be much more effective if you put yourself into that mindset first. Clear yourself of unfinished business now, clearing the way and freeing you to take advantage of the new opportunities that will come about at the new Moon.

The Waning Moon is associated with the Crone aspect of the Goddess. Now is also the time for you to engage in those activities which increase your own wisdom. Think of a plan and begin to act on it. This cycle of the Moon can be just as powerful and productive as any of the other Moon phases, or it can be a time of decreased activity and increased rest. It's all up to you.

Lunar Journal: Waning Moon

Honor your existence. Be aware of the smells around you, the creatures and the plants, the tastes of all you eat and the dreams that fill your idle time. Grant yourself time to live this day in many dimensions.

What do you see when you look past the ordinary?

Do you experience difference between completion and ending?

What kinds of dreams are you having? Are you remembering them when you wake?

Waning Moon

As the Moon wanes toward those final days of darkness. we often feel a need to turn inward. The Sun and the Moon are once again squared to each other. This is the end of the cycle and is a good time for completing or eliminating anything that is no longer necessary. It is a time to mentally clean our house.

Unwanted habits and other negative influences should be cast away at this time. Some bad habits...such as smoking...can be extremely hard to break so here it is best to set a realistic time frame. Utilize this time for banishing or manifestations to get rid of unwanted or stuck energy.

It is also a time to share the accomplishments of the preceding Waxing Moon, to reap what we have sown as well as weed and prune what we don't need in order to clear the way for the new energy. This is the Goddess as Crone....She is elder and wise....the Goddess of the Crossroads. Because She no longer bleeds, She retains Her power. She is the knower of mysteries, of the secrets of existence, of things that are hidden. She presides in the dream world and guides us through the unconscious labyrinth of our minds.

Discovering the Waning Gibbous Moon

A Waning gibbous Moon sails over the eastern horizon in the hours between sunset and midnight.

The Moon is past full now. Once again, it appears less than full but more than half lighted.

What can I say about a Waning gibbous Moon? Only that it can surprise you if you happen to be out late in the evening. It rises eerily some hours after sunset, glowing red like a full Moon when it's near the horizon. Sometimes it looks like a misshapen clone of a full Moon. Because it comes up late at night, the Waning gibbous Moon prompts people to start asking, "Where is the Moon? I looked for it last night and couldn't find it."

The Waning gibbous Moon also initiates a rash of questions about seeing the Moon during the day. If it rises late at night, you know the Waning gibbous Moon must set after sunrise. In fact, in the few days after full Moon, you'll often see the Waning gibbous Moon in the West in early morning, floating against the pale blue sky.

Knowing the Waning Gibbous Moon

In astrology the Waning Gibbous Moon is called disseminating. The Full Moon has passed, though just barely. She still lights up the night sky, and the darkness of earth, although she is visibly Waning. The Waning phase is primarily about endings and letting go, in contrast to the beginnings and growth of the Waxing phase. It's time to begin letting go, to realize that a transformation is needed before there can be further growth.

We have made the transition from Waxing to Waning, like stepping through a doorway, and now it's time to see what awaits us. In fact, through out the busy cycle this is the first time we have really stopped to look around. We begin to see where we stand, and notice our surroundings and our place in them. The disseminating phase is integrative. Our awareness of others, their needs and goals, their effect on us is heightened. We begin to see where our knowledge may be useful to others, and their knowledge may be useful to us. The visions began at New Moon, the fulfillment gained at Full Moon, the experiences in-between have began transforming into wisdom and understanding. We are compelled to share it. We absorb what others have to share. Communication is vital.

Following the natural path of the Moon, it is time to take a step back. Not a step backwards in progress, but step back from situations you are too close to, look at them objectively. From the darkness of New Moon, she has progressed, grown, increased to the peak of Full Moon. Now she is gracefully and slowly slipping into the shadows. She is revisiting the darkness. Dark does not mean evil or bad. Knowledge, wisdom, understanding, and subconscious all live in the quiet depths of the shadows. Begin turning your attention to things of this nature.

This is only the beginning of the Waning portion of the Lunar Cycle. We begin by seeking understanding. At Full Moon, things are illuminated, accomplished, goals are reached, ideas are solidified. Now we know. But do we understand? The mind is busy, sharing and gathering information, racing with thoughts. This is the time to process those thoughts, bits of information, memories of experiences into wisdom and a valuable tool you can use for the rest of this cycle, and all that follow it.

The sharing of information is one of the critical elements of, and uses for the Disseminating Phase. If you have a message to get out, now is the time. If others are talking (about something relevant) listen to what they have to say. Study, learn, and absorb ideas and information. The tendency for sharing and interaction is not limited to information, although that is its primary influence. This can be an excellent time for socializing, teaching children to share, charity work. It's perfect for attending (or teaching) classes and workshops, making friends whom you connect to on an intellectual level, or exploring other cultures. Learn and diversify, keep an open mind.

This phase is usually a busy time (at least mentally), but in the rush to share, gain, and digest ideas don't forget that the general tendency of the Waning phase is decreasing and letting go. This is a good time for breaking habits, changing routines, and weeding out ideas which aren't useful. Be open to change, as this phase is a beginning of a transformation. Ask yourself what you need to transform.

Now that we are in the Waning phase it is no longer favorable to begin projects for growth and increase, because the natural tendency is decreasing. The disseminating phase has a strong focus on information. If you want to get a message out, 'spread the word' this is a perfect time. It's also a good time for gathering information. Think ahead to what you have planned for the next Waxing Moon, and do your research. If you are in the middle of a big project or a difficult/confusing situation or point in your life ask yourself what you need to know. Information is a powerful tool, and if you don't have all the facts, or don't fully understand them use this time to remedy the situation. By the same merit if your side of the story hasn't been heard - tell it.

The Disseminating Phase also marks the beginning of transformation. Think change. Even in things we want to progress and grow, the balance of Waning is essential. Do you have a stalled project, or feel stuck in a rut? Then something has to change, opening new doors, giving new options. Something has to end making room for new growth, or allowing it to be 'reborn' in a different and better way.

LUNAR JOURNAL: WANING MOON

- Change your goals from outer achievements to the attainment of inner peace.

- Meditate, rest and try to spend some time in nature....alone...or listen to music.

- Let go; release old beliefs, possessions and relationships that no longer work for you.

Moon Mirror Healing

Place a silvered mirror, face up on an altar or other sacred place so that the light of the Waning Moon shines upon it. In the center of the mirror, place a symbol to represent the one seeking healing. The symbol could be a photo, crystal, lit candle, piece of jewelry, lock of hair, name on a card, or some other object.

Use the symbol on the mirror in the Moonlight as a focal point as you imagine that the one needing healing is becoming well and then is healthy. After the ritual, deliver the symbol to the subject of the healing rite as an additional way of transmitting healing.

Cleanse the mirror you used by washing it with salt water or passing it through sage smoke or some other incense so that the mirror will be ready for you to use for other healing work in the future.

Understanding the Last Quarter

A last quarter Moon looks half-illuminated. It rises around midnight, appears at its highest in the sky at dawn, and sets around noon.

Last quarter Moon comes about three weeks after New Moon. Now, as seen from above, the Moon in its orbit around Earth is at right angles to a line between the Earth and sun. The Moon is now three-quarters of the way around in its orbit of Earth, as measured from one new Moon to the next.

It's very cool to see the last quarter Moon just after it rises, around midnight. The image at the top of this post illustrates it well. Just after the last quarter Moon rises, its lighted portion is always facing downwards, reasonably toward the horizon. Why? Because you're on the midnight portion of Earth – with the sun below your feet – just as it's below this Moon.

After the last quarter phase, the Moon will begin edging noticeably closer to the sun again on the sky's dome. Fewer people notice the Moon during the day from about last quarter on, because the sun's glare begins to dominate the Moon.

A last quarter Moon can be used as a guidepost to Earth's direction of motion in orbit around the sun. In other words, when you look at a last quarter Moon high in the predawn sky, you're gazing out approximately along the path of Earth's orbit, in a forward direction. The Moon is moving in orbit around the sun with the Earth. But, if we could somehow anchor the Moon in space . . . tie it down, keep it still . . . Earth's orbital speed of 18 miles per second would carry us across the space between us and the Moon in only a few hours.

Knowing the Last Quarter

Once again we have reached the balance of light. The Moon begins this phase exactly half illuminated, but Waning. She is slipping into the darkness, slowly but surely. Each night we see another sliver of light gone. She still illuminates the night, but gradually the shadows grow stronger and the light grows weaker. It is a time of transition, transformation, and evolution. There is a restless, sometimes uneasy feeling. Instinctively we feel that something is happening, something is changing.

In the First Quarter Phase we feel the energy of Waxing and growing become quite potent at the light overtakes the dark. We have now reached the opposite point, as the dark overtakes the light and we feel the energy of Waning and decreasing with equal potency. However, the darkness is the quiet, the internal, the letting go, the understanding, it is a more subtle energy. The mysteries of the shadows are now more alluring than the discoveries of the light. The energy is deep and powerful, but not so easy to decipher as the extroverted and illuminating energy we felt in the First Quarter.

Half light, half dark. We are looking back, and looking ahead. Often we find ourselves at a crossroads during the Last Quarter Phase, sometimes trying to (or needing to) take both roads at once. Things began early in the phase are coming to fruition. There are things that still need to be done, perhaps another big push to finish up. Maybe they should be continued, or revived. It's decision time. Then, there is the question of where to from here. What will replace things that have been finished? What will be started in the next phase? Again, decision time.

Look back: where have you been, and what have you done? Look ahead: where are you going, and what will you do? This is a time of change, as we are beginning to form plans for the future, realizing the repercussions of the past, and deciding what we will (or must) continue, and bring with us. This isn't a time to dodge responsibility and avoid decisions. We often find ourselves facing mistakes we have made, and receiving credit for what we have archived. We become aware of what is finished, or needs to be. We've been gathering wisdom, contemplating change. Now we begin to figure out what to do with what we have, and don't have.

The Quarter Moon Phases, both first and last, are times of balance followed by direction. This one is vastly different from the First Quarter, however. This is a good time to break bad habits and change routines. Sometimes the more stubborn habits are easier to break now than in the Disseminating Phase. There is sometimes a vague feeling of chaos in our lives around this time. Be careful not to let things spin out of control, but don't be too concerned. It's natural, this is a turning point and there are probably many things going on simultaneously. Don't let yourself slip into bad habits, and not do what has to be done. However, don't push yourself too hard either. Rest and contemplation is integral to the entire Waning phase.

The Last Quarter Phase is a good time for taking care of details. Do things you've been putting off. Clean out the closet, finish up some paperwork. Work on wrapping things up, and deal with those 'odds and ends' you've been neglecting. It's a good time to organize, prioritize, streamline, and weed out. Clean up clutter, throw away things you don't need and make room for those 'homeless' things laying around.

This can be an important point in long-term projects and goals. This is a time for making the hard decisions, and implementing serious change. What needs to be eliminated? If you are have come to a point where you must choose one of two (or more) directions, this is a good time to make your choice. Now is the time for restructuring, and reconsidering plans. Take a hard look at what has and hasn't worked, make use of information you've gathered. This is a time of endings, but not always eliminating things. This is a good time for finishing, or beginning the final stage of something. If you have a project near completion, it can be a good time to take the necessary steps to finish it; make time and room for something new.

Mistakes made along the way may, and problems you've encountered be catching up with you. Don't ignore them, or give up on what you've been trying to do. See what there is to be learned, and how they may be avoided in the future. Implement change where needed, or use this time to figure out what change is needed. Take a hones look at projects, or things in your life that seem to be going downhill. Decide if it's worth pursuing or not. There is a difference in giving up, depressed, frustrated, and illogical or thinking it through and deciding that it's not worth continuing with. Decide weather you're ending the goal or the plan. If you're ending the plan, but the goal is still worth striving for, consider a new start, a different approach, in the coming Lunar Cycle.

If you're ending the goal, do what is needed to wrap it up, and start thinking ahead. Consider the possibilities opened up by the time and resources you're freeing up.

Lunar Journal: The Last Quarter

This is a time of focusing energy on the task at hand, or, if we try to avoid this, we might find ourselves confronted by others; this can mean that things can begin going 'right' for us with progress made, or it can mean that things begin going 'wrong' for us--something breaks down on us, people give up on us or gives us problems, things become impossible. Either way, we are now faced with the truth of how we fit into our world, and the outcomes of our acts to date stand before us.

Although we like to think of ourselves as independent, in reality, our lives are in a great degree in the hands of others...and if we have been acting is if we were a victim, we can suffer at this time. What is done is done? The past is beginning to end and a glimmer of the future peeks out at us. At the New Moon, the future is reborn as a seed of possibilities for a future cycle.

We all have a role which we have either accepted or rejected and a question pops up before us. What have I gotten from all of this, and where will it lead me in the end?

Discovering the Waning Crescent

A Waning crescent Moon is sometimes called an old Moon. It's seen in the East before dawn. Now the Moon has moved nearly entirely around in its orbit of Earth, as measured from one new Moon to the next. Because the Moon is nearly on a line with the Earth and sun again, the day hemisphere of the Moon is facing mostly away from us again. We see only a slender fraction of the Moon's day side: a crescent Moon.

Each morning before dawn, because the Moon is moving eastward in orbit around Earth, the Moon appears closer to the sunrise glare. We see less and less of the Moon's day side, and thus the crescent in the East before dawn appears thinner each day. The Moon, as always, is rising in the East day after day. But most people won't see this Moon phase unless they get up early. When the sun comes up, and the sky grows brighter, the Waning crescent Moon fades. Now the Moon is so near the Earth/sun line that the sun's glare is drowning this slim Moon from view.

Still, the Waning crescent is up there, nearly all day long, moving ahead of the sun across the sky's dome. It sets in the West several hours or less before sunset.

KNOWING THE WANING CRESCENT MOON

The darkness is nearly complete. We begin the Waning Crescent Phase with just a thin sliver of light - you may catch a glimpse in early morning - and by the end of the phase, darkness is complete. We are approaching Dark Moon; this is the last Waning phase. She has withdrawn into the darkness, leaving the night wrapped in shadows. Disappearing from sight, she is resting, preparing for the next Lunar Cycle. As we follow her example, follow her path, we do the same.

This is a time of quiet contemplation. We withdraw into the shadowy depths of thought and emotion, resting, reflecting, thinking, feeling, dreaming, and preparing. To a great degree we exist in the 'invisible worlds' of subconscious, spiritual realms, daydreaming, and our own inner depths. We are often consciously unaware, much is happening, yet it seems that nothing is happening. The past slips away, quietly into the night as the future slips in. While the Moon releases her current cycle, extinguishing the light and preparing for the next cycle, we to are releasing extinguishing and preparing; even if we don't know it on a conscious level.

This is a time to notice the subtle, especially within yourself. It's not a time of dramatic changes and hectic action. Yet it's a time of chaos, in it's own way. There is often an uneasy, restlessness about the Waning Crescent

Phase. This isn't typically chaos in the external sense, of noticeable disorder and confusion. This is a deeper, more subtle more meaningful type of chaos. The Lunar cycle is ending, with it our cycle of progress and action is ending. Yet a new cycle has not begun. There is a sense of void, but it's not a void. It's filled with the past, the future, hopes and fears. Externally this should be a calm, quiet time. Allow yourself opportunity to think, feel and experience.

The Waning Crescent Moon Phase is a time of release. The growing and building of the Waxing phase have passes. The actively analyzing, correcting, and changing of the Waning phase up to this point has passes. Now is the time for acceptance and release. What has gone too far to be repairable, we must let go of? Perhaps it will be restarted in the next, or a future Lunar Cycle. Maybe it won't. But if it's time has come, we must now let go. We must have faith in ourselves, and the natural cycle, knowing what we let go of now will be reborn, the resources will be reused, we are making way for something new, releasing emotions and beginning healing...

Waning Crescent Moon is also a time of preparation. New Moon is approaching; we are on the verge of the next Lunar Cycle. We are on the verge, but not there yet. Gather your strength and resources; let your mind and body relax. Let your spirit and soul play. Let your imagination run wild. We are following the natural cycle. The Moon is now retreating into the shadows, withdrawing into herself, resting and preparing to come back strong and vibrant in the next cycle. This is the time we should be preparing ourselves to be refreshed and ready for great momentum and new growth to come.

One of the best uses for the Waning Crescent Phase is rest. If you've been pushing yourself too hard, feeling used up and burnt out, the most important thing to do right now is give yourself a break. It's also a time to get in touch either yourself and nature. This is the time to stop and smell the roses, enjoy the moment. It's also a good time for mundane, routine tasks, the kind of thing you do automatically without having to give it much though. Try to avoid strenuous activities, especially mentally strenuous. This is the time for your mind to relax, and let your subconscious, your soul, and your imagination flow. Don't fill your head with a group of fact and figures, that won't let the subtle flow through.

For more 'practical' activities, remember we are in the final days of the Waning Moon. It won't be favorable time for breaking habits, endings, or eliminating until the next phase. If you have things of this nature you need to do, now is the time. This phase of the Waning Moon is particularly good for final endings. Anything you don't want to return, or want it to at least be slower than typical, now is the time. For example, if you pull weeds they don't grow back as quickly, if you clean out the junk drawer, it will fill up slower, if you plug a leak it's more likely to hold and so on.

Reflecting Lunar Pools

What to do:
Place the bowl of water on the table. Relax. Imagine your image in the bowl of water, allow the brightness of the Moon to wash over your reflection. Visualize this for a few minutes. Take your finger and poke it in the waters semi hard, rippling the waters.

Say:
*"Lunar waters cleanse and the waters calm
My mind and heart from this emotional storm."*

Repeat this over and over again until the water is totally unrippled while visualizing yourself within the water being happy and emotionally balanced. Empty the water bowl out.

V
THE DARK MOON
One Night Only
Day 28

Is the Moon tired? She looks so pale
Within her misty veil:
She scales the sky from east to west,
And takes no rest.
Before the coming of the night
The Moon shows papery white;
Before the dawning of the day
She fades away.
—Christina G. Rossetti

The dark Moon appears in the sky during the last day of every lunar cycle, and during this time, the night is without Moonlight, but the Dark Moon is there; it is the Dark Moon that presides over the sky until the new 28-day cycle begins, and a New Moon is ready to appear. Sometimes referred to as the "Dead Moon," the Dark Moon doesn't necessarily represent death. It is, however, a powerful time. It seems to lure us toward the deepest self, the longings of our soul.

When the Dark Moon appears, it becomes easier for us to shed unnecessary emotional baggage and let go of those people and ideas that no longer serve us or add value to our life. It is a time to cleanse ourselves and create space so that what is new can enter. The dark of the Moon comes with a pull inward, and for many people, this is a time to rest, reflect, and replenish their energy. It is an excellent time for deep meditation and going within, understanding, and gaining knowledge of self. During this Moon cycle many have reported having powerful healing dreams, and it is at this time that most people feel driven to explore their intuitive abilities, retrieve past life memories, or delve more deeply into their psyche.

This is a time to perform manifestations for prophecy, cursing or chaos, but of course, if one curses another, they shall reap what they have sown. Black is the main color of Crone magic. Black is a color of which many are fearful for it signifies the absence of color....yet, it encompasses all of the colors. It dispels negative energy quickly and is very good for banishing manifestations.

One way to harness the energy of the Dark Moon is to perform a ritual. Begin by lighting a black candle and calling forth those different parts of your life that you feel you are ready to let go of. Through visualization, bind these parts together with light and imagine the bundle moving toward the candle. Watch as these old parts are devoured by the flames. Finally, let the candle burn out. Trust that what you've released has left you. You are now ready to welcome the new into your life.

Lunar Journal: Dark Moon Release

We are now at the phase to release ourselves, let go of things that seem to not bring our lives into alignment.

This is a time of great introspection as we manifest the life we want? Ask yourself the following questions:

- When the Moon was full we saw unlimited potential, what might be missing?

- What or who no longer serve me, and why?

- What seemingly negative thing will I actively choose to see as a positive?

Manifesting Change

The Dark of the Moon, a mysterious time of 'molding' the creative experiences that will come forth in the weeks ahead, is almost here. This is a powerful time, a time of quiet and reflection. This period of the Moon is always best used to rest, recuperate, become quite, invite calm and serenity into your world and to spend some time in personal reflection of your life and personal history. Where do you want to go from here? Create the conditions that will replenish your spirit and indulge them fully...whether this means reading, journal writing, meditation, listening to music...whatever works for you.

The Dark of the Moon is a time of legendary power for creation. This is a time to play with ideas and think of things you might like to create over the next several weeks. Brainstorm. Daydream. But, this is not the time to take action. Remember that all things begin in the mind. Remember, everything in the world originated from an idea, a dream, a desire.

Dark Moon Rising

The Moon continues to grow small, and soon, very soon, it will have waned completely, and we will find that it appears to have vanished completely. This is why it is called the "Dark Moon" or the "Dead Moon." It signifies death, but not literally a physical death, but because it is because this is the last cycle of the Moon, and there will be no Moon for us to see...because the Moon is now conjunct the Sun...rising at sunrise and setting at sunset. To the ancients, this was a symbol of death. Some people just don't even deal with this period of the Dark Moon which lasts for approximately three days...the day before, the day of the "New Moon," and the day after. This is when the power of the Moon is at its weakest. But, I believe this is a very important phase.

For many, and this is important for those of us who feel drained, this is a time of rest and introspection where little or no magical workings are done. This is where we give ourselves a much needed break, to turn to self and to pamper and replenish our energies.

Yet, some traditions hold that the Dark Moon holds the same power as the Full Moon. The Goddess has turned her face away from us, and darkness walks the earth. For those in these traditions, dark energies are conjured during this time; it is a time for black magic and dark working.

The keyword for this cycle of the Moon are solitude, introspection, divination, rest, and resurrection.

Throughout time, the Moon has long been associated with our power within, and men, as well as women, are capable of connecting with this power. The dark phase, which is associated with the crone phase, appears in the sky during the last three days of every lunar cycle; it is a time for life-enriching endings and a prelude to new beginnings. When the dark Moon appears to us, we find it much easier to shed that unnecessary emotional baggage which we carry within us and to free ourselves of those people and ideas that no longer add value to our life. This is the time when we need to cleanse ourselves of the old and unnecessary to create space so that the new can enter.

One way that we can harness the energy of the dark Moon is to perform a simple ritual where you light a black candle. Black candles open up the deeper levels of the unconscious and are good for banishing evil or negativity from your life. Call forth and visualize the different parts of your life that you are ready to let go of. Then, through visualization, bind these parts together with light and imagine that this bundle is moving toward the candle. Watch as these parts are devoured by the flame; then let the candle burn out. Trust that what you have released has now left you.

A Solitary Dark Moon Ritual

For this ritual you will need two black candles, a cauldron, paper, and a pen.

First, place the cauldron in the center of your altar; then place the paper and the pen next to it. Now, cast the circle in a counter-clockwise way, and once it is cast, return to your altar and face towards the North. While lighting the black candles say:

"This is the time when the dark Moon hides Her face from humans. Oh, Dark Mother, oh Wise One, let me feel Your presence and Your power. I need Your wisdom of releasing and removing."

Move counter-clockwise to the East and say:

Dark Mother, remove all of the negatives from my thoughts and mind and let them bear no fruit within my life.

Part II

DRAWING DOWN THE MOON
Invoking the Myths

If that which you seek, you find not within yourself
you will never find it without.
For behold, I have been with you from the Beginning, and
I am that which is attained at the end of desire.
  - Charge of the Goddess

Drawing down the Moon is an amazing experience where you draw the power of the Moon inside you, as well as invoking the Goddess inside of you. It's a very beautiful and powerful experience. Let me break it down for you a little bit more.

The time of the full Moon is a very magical and powerful time. This is the perfect time for big manifestations that you need quick results from. But the most important part of it is this: at the time of the full Moon, magic reaches it's peak of the month for drawing things to you. After the full Moon, you go into the

Waning phase. During the Moon's Waning phase it is best to do manifestations that send things away from you such as banishing and releasing. During the Waning phase, many witches notice that their powers seem to dwindle a little bit as well. Ever noticed how around the time of the Waning Moon you seem a little sluggish and tired? No? Well, maybe that's just me. However, because of the Waning phase of the Moon, things are diminishing and decreasing, so when you have a full Moon, drawing down the Moon will help you store up extra energy.

. During the Waxing Moon we have all sorts of energy and are capable of storing up more energy. During the Waning Moon, we can become a little sluggish and seem to be diminishing energy.

Drawing down the full Moon. The full Moon is like when the sun is at it's full peak with your solar battery storing even more energy from it. So, we draw down the Moon to keep a well of energy stored during the Waxing phase to use for any of our manifestation work t

So how do we go about doing that? Well, my friends, I have a little ritual that I like to do from time to time. As I stated before, it's been years since I've done this, but this is a tried and true ritual!

Drawing Down the Moon

Supplies
Drinking glass
Water
Incense
Salt
Candle

The incense can be any scent that you feel called to. The candle would be perfect if it were silver, but sometimes silver candles are hard to come across, so a white candle will do as well. You don't have to have a huge candle, it can be a tea light, but some people do like having one large candle, dedicated to full Moon work, that you light only during their full Moon rituals.

If the weather allows it, go outside where you can see the full Moon in absolute plain sight. If it's raining or just too darn cold, or your neighbors might freak out, it's fine to do this ritual inside. If working inside, make sure you are near a window where you can get full view of the Moon.

Now, once you've decided where you are going to do your ritual, it's time to set up a ritual sacred space. Make sure you have a flat surface to set your candle, bowl of salt, incense, and glass of water on.

CASTING THE CIRCLE:

Give yourself lots of room to work. You don't want to feel confined to a tiny space, so don't just stand in one place and turn around in a circle, walk a large circle. If you're inside your home, and have just a small space to work at, like myself, you can envision a circle forming around your entire home. If working outside, walk a largish circle around your altar/workspace.

While walking the circle, walk in a clockwise motion, and you can point with your finger to create this circle. As you are walking clockwise, envision a magical boundary appearing and covering your workspace in a big bubble.

Say: *"As this circle opens, all negativity is kept at bay. Only those invited within this circle may enter, and may only come with an open heart."*

Then when I see the circle complete itself, I'll walk to the middle and say, "As above, so below, this circle is now open."

With you're circle is open, and you have a safe place to work. Now you're probably wondering what to do next. That's pretty easy. Remember where you started walking your circle?

Using your salt, and go there. Walk the circle again and toss a little salt as you walk saying, "By the power of earth, this circle is protected." Next grab your water, and walk the circle, saying, "By the power of water, this circle is protected." Use the incense, light it, and walk the circle saying, "By the power of air, this circle is protected." Light the candle, walk with it around the circle saying, "By the power of fire, this circle is protected."

Now you're circle is completely protected and ready to go!

Walk to your altar, gaze up at the Moon. Now say:

Goddess of the Moon, full, beautiful, and fair. Please enter into this circle with me.

Envision the pure silver light of Moonlight tunneling into your circle, filling it, but not blinding. Feel the goddess standing beside you. Now, hold your glass of water above your head, facing the Moon. Envision that same silver light filling the glass and swirling through the water. Envision the silver light overflowing the glass. Feel the energy tingle through the glass, through your fingertips, and into you. Now say:

Goddess of the Moon, I ask that you fill my glass with your pure energy.

As the water turns into your energy, I ask that you sustain me through all the days to come.

Now drink the water. Feel the energy coursing through your body. Let it swirl throughout every part of your body. Envision it filling you with silver light from your toes to the crown of your head. When it reaches the crown of your head, let it spill out in a straight line, back to the Moon, connecting you with the Goddess of the Moon.

Envision your toes as roots, and meditate momentarily on how the Moon sustains the earth, and all that live in it. Once you've finished, feel the energy, and everywhere that it has touched within your body. By now, your body is probably tingling all over, and it may be hard for you to focus, which is totally normal. Pull the energy from your fingers, toes, and head, down into the center of your belly. Feel it's warmth and strength there. This is where you will carry the energy until the next time you draw down the Moon.

Now that you've centered the energy, there will probably be excess, and you may feel a bit light headed, or dizzy, or even just super amped. If you are outside, sit on the ground, and let the excess energy flow into the ground.

Do not let the energy in your center flow out, only the excess that is buzzing around everywhere else. Now is the perfect time to talk with Goddess, cast any manifestations you had planned for tonight, or just be at peace inside your circle. Once you've finished whatever you planned, you can close the circle.

Walk counterclockwise, watching the circle disappear. Thank the Goddess for all of her blessings, and for sharing her energy with you before closing the circle. You can let the incense burn down, put out your candle, and clean up the area. Now that everything is cleaned up, it would probably be a good idea for you to have something to eat. Even after grounding (when you sat on the ground and let the excess energy flow into it), you are probably going to feel a little off in some way. Eating something will help fully bring you back to this world, and fully ground you.

THE TRIPLE MOON GODDESS: MAIDEN, MOTHER AND CRONE

The first face of the Moon goddess, the crescent Moon, is her Maiden aspect, representing youthfulness, expectancy, innocence, newness. She is the dawn, enchantment, seduction and fruitfulness. Through her eyes, we see the freshness and beauty of life and hold reverence and wonder in our hearts. She is open to all experiences for she is unafraid of the unknown.

The Maiden is also called the Virgin. Many of the ancient goddesses were virgin goddesses. A virgin was a woman who 'belonged to no man', a young woman who was unmarried. Possibly this is the meaning of Mary being a virgin when she conceived Jesus. Esther Harding's work on women's mysteries suggests that to be a virgin means to be 'one-in-herself', a woman who accepts her own sovereignty. It did not mean a young woman who is sexually inexperienced. To be virginal means being true to nature and to your instincts rather than giving over to another's needs or demands. Virginity is a creative submission to the demands of instinct, rather than a rejection or denial of those instincts.9   Virgin forests are not barren places, but rather ones that are especially fruitful, for they are unexploited and still totally natural. How many of us, whether woman or man, know how to be virginal in this sense?

The virgin acts according to her own nature. She gives herself to lovers but is never possessed by them; she is never just the counterpart of a male, either god or man. In ancient Greece, this aspect of the Moon was honored as Artemis, goddess of wild things, and leader of the Dance. This Virgin Goddess watched over childbirth and was the womb opener10 because childbirth demands that we surrender to instinctual rhythms. In surrendering to her instinctual nature, a woman becomes creative.

Each month, a woman can become virginal again with each new shedding of menstrual blood which prepares the womb for new life. At this time, a woman stands grounded in her instincts, ready with her creative potential to meet the demands of her life. This stage represents young women through their 20's, as they go out into the world to work and to prove themselves in the world. This is a time of adventure and exploration, when we learn how to listen to our own natures and learn to be free.

Psychologically, the crescent Moon is an image this new beginning. It stands as a sign of psychic energy emerging out of the darkness of the unconscious, continually evolving, continuing to bring us new life experiences. Each month the new crescent Moon stands in the western sky at sunset, shining with fragile beauty, evoking a feeling of hope and new life to come. It is during this part of the Moon cycle that we experience a sense of expectancy, for who knows what experiences are waiting for us. It evokes our youthful sense of independence and individuality that sometimes gets lost in the midst of our hectic lives. Our bodies, our emotions and our thoughts can open to new possibilities, where we think outside the box, start new projects, and permit ourselves new feelings.

As the Moon comes to its fullness, it fully turns to meet the light of the Sun. This second aspect of the Moon is the Mother, a stage that represents the creation and ripening of life, the state of adulthood and parenthood. It is the time to take responsibility for yourself and others, to learn the lessons of patience and self-discipline. As the nurturing mother, this stage knows and teaches the mysteries of Life, just as a mother teaches her children how to grow up to be good human beings. This is the stage where we learn the power of Love as an exchange, the energy that connects us to others.

We first learn to love ourselves in the Maiden stage so we can learn to love others in the Mother stage. One without the other doesn't work, because if we can't love ourselves, we won't know how to love someone else.

We must be grounded in self-love to do everything. This self-love comes to us through honoring our instinctive knowing.

A mother's love is unconditional and compassionate, and yet not without discipline. We nurture our children to teach them the mysteries of life, and sometimes that means not giving them what they think they need, but letting them learn how to get it for themselves. The mother has the wisdom of life at her core, and she teaches this wisdom by example as well as through any creative endeavor she takes up. The care and nurturing she gives her children, both outer and inner, is reflected in the strength and truth of those creations. Full Moon consciousness nurtures the newly born baby, a new behavior, a new creative project or a relationship in the same way – with love and devotion.

In ancient Greece, Hera was worshiped as the Moon, and as the Full Moon in particular. Although the patriarchy gave her the thankless role of the jealous wife, she originally embodied the power of the union of opposites, the power that comes from the sacred marriage of masculine and feminine energies. As the full Moon, She was known as the Perfect One, and Zeus, Her consort, was called the Perfector.

Her virginal aspect was not lost but brought to its perfection by union with the Other. From the myths, we know that the patriarchal mind could not allow women to own their sovereignty, and so this mighty goddess became a stereotype for patriarchal marriage. We can see why in Greek mythology Hera gets so terribly angry with Zeus' sexual escapades, for he does not allow her to be true to her nature as the Perfect One. He refused to complete her. When we are in relationship, we can neither lose ourselves in it nor hold back from it. True relationship is about incorporating two different yet complementary energies, completing each other.

Psychologically, this full Moon experience is the 'rounding out' of an idea, a desire or a feeling by coming into relationship with others or bringing it into the world in some creative fashion. This full Moon consciousness can look at an ego decision, which thinks there is only one truth, and show it another, equally viable, way to see things. It can hold both ideas until the third, transcendent path opens.

A young woman dreamed: I am looking at the sky at night together with my mother. I see two huge full Moons and I tell my mom how amazing that is and that it is not possible. My mother tells me that she has no glasses and she can't see it. Somehow I have her old glasses with me and I give them to her and she can see everything clearly.

This woman can suddenly see both side of the issue. It's her inner mother who isn't sure she can see both sides. Our mothers can only give us what they know. And so sometimes we have to show them the way. Like Persephone, this dreamer knows something that she has to share with her mother. Something awesome, something new. A larger, more feminine consciousness. Perhaps her mother, like Allerleirauh's mother, can't get beyond her patriarchal mindset without her daughter's help.

Women in their 30's and 40's are in this stage of life. This is the time of motherhood and marriage, where we learn to partner and to parent. We become involved in our schools and our communities as we help our children grow into adulthood. This is when we learn to work with a partner toward a common goal. It is a time when we can be perfected in our sense of ourselves. To really meet the Other entails an openness, a willingness to be totally present in yourself for the Other; it entails an ability to allow new perceptions or awareness so we can meet the world without retreating back to the stability of old habits or values.

In the story, Allerleirauh experiences this full Moon openness when she appears at the balls. She goes to the festival openly, dressed in splendor, ready to meet the king on her own terms. This is the hardest part - to be in relationship without losing our sense of self. This is the point when we need the Moon's virtues of spirit, heart and courage, for it takes a firm belief in ourselves and the spirit within to meet the demands of life in this way. If women can learn to keep this sense of self in the midst of being in relationship, we will heal the wounds that break our marriages apart. For relationships are in the hands of women, not men, and it is one of the ways we can bring about the change that is needed in the world and between men and women.

The third aspect, the Waning Moon, represents the Crone or Wise Woman. This was the most feared, least understood aspect of the Moon goddess. This is the aspect that was called the Hag, the Terrible Mother, the Witch, the Wise One. This aspect of the cycle deals with death, the end of cycles, and the mysteries surrounding re-birth. The more we fear old age, death, and the unknown, the more we fear this aspect of the cycle. But if we can accept this part of the cycle, we will find the treasure of wisdom that we've been seeking: the wisdom that sustains life, the wisdom to evolve our consciousness.

The Crone, whose name means crown, symbolizes the achievement of Wisdom culled from the experience of loving and nurturing that we learned at the full Moon as well as the wisdom of the Virgin who knows herself. Just as we find a peace and harmony within as we grow older - as the fire and impatience of youth is felt but is no longer overwhelming to us - so too the Waning Moon is a time of introversion and withdrawal. It teaches us to be alone with ourselves. It teaches when it's time to let go and let the old die. It is a time to realize what we understand and the wisdom that comes from that knowledge.

No one would ever mistake the Waning Moon for the Waxing Moon, for there is a wholly different feel to each of them. I am always struck by the beauty of the Waxing crescent, which fills me with hope and excitement, whereas the Waning crescent rising after midnight always leaves me with a feeling of mystery, of being far away and alone. You can tell the light is sinking toward death.

This is the aspect that was worshiped – and later feared - as Hecate. In ancient Greece, the power of the Moon also belonged to the goddess Hecate. She was called, like the Moon itself, the 'most lovely' and had three aspects: Hecate Selene, the Moon in heaven,

Artemis the Huntress on earth and Persephone the Destroyer in the underworld. Hecate originated in Egypt, where she was the midwife or wise woman, who commanded 'the mother's Words of Power'.

The Greeks finally came to worship her as the Crone who guarded the triple crossroads, the central axis where the different worlds meet. She held the powers of prophecy and magic, as well as the ability to commune with the dead.

We no longer fear, as later Christians did, Hecate as the goddess of magic, for we know that magic is the power to see the energies of life and direct them with our will, not necessarily the work of evil powers. It can be used for evil, but that depends on the person. We create magic when we use the power of intention and ritual to enhance our lives.

This is Crone energy, and it represents the power and wisdom of Moon consciousness. Women in their 50's and older begin to feel comfortable with this energy, and as healers and wise women they bring healing to their families, their communities and to the world.

It is the wisdom that facing death can bestow, the energy which sinks into the darkness of the new Moon, the psychic energy that sinks back into the unconscious to be renewed. The old life must pass away so that new life can come. The wisdom is not lost in that darkness but rather transformed, so that it becomes part of the new virginal energy which re-appears at the crescent Moon once again. With each new cycle, we add to our understanding and go deeper within the mysteries of life.

The Goddess also has a fourth aspect, the dark and hidden side of her nature. This is the mystery, her death aspect, the time of her descent into the underworld, the time of the dark of the Moon. In ancient Greece, this dark side of the Moon was ruled by Persephone, the Queen of the Dead, the guardian of the treasures of the underworld. It is why she is also the Spring Maiden, for she comes back to the outer world with the gifts she has wrestled from the darkness of the unknown. The fact that this Goddess was worshiped as life-giving and death-dealing shows that these aspects cannot be separated. But since we have separated them, the terror of death is ever with us.

The ancients worshiped this Goddess through the initiation of the Eleusinian Mysteries, which gave them the immediate experience of a death and rebirth which helped them to accept the terror of death and separation from their old life. It is this initiation that we have to undergo if we want to experience the power of feminine wholeness.

GODDESS OF THE MOON

The Moon as Goddess is a common theme in many cultures. Two that stand out most to me, are the Chinese Chang-O and also the Mayan IxChel. I have adapted their mysteries here, and offer them as reflection to how two civilizations seemingly with no connection turned to the Moon for understanding and reflection.

These two stories invite us to look at what the Moon represents and invites with it a dialogue with the Feminine dive. After each story is a ritual that helps you to manifest the lesson in the lore.

Your Lunar Journal invitation is to write how these stories impacted you, and if you feel them in more than just the words. Do you resonate with one more than the other? Have there been moments in your worn life where you see an overlap with either Chang-O or IxChel?

Chang-O

Ch'ang-O also called Chang'e is the Chinese Goddess of the Moon. She does not personify the moon like other moon goddesses. She lives on the moon and is sometimes called the "Woman on the Moon".

Cha'ngo and how she came to live on the moon has many stories in Chinese mythology and variations. One story is that Ch'ang-O was a young immortal girl working in the palace of Heaven for the Jade Emperor. One day she accidentally broke a valuable porcelain jar in the palace and the Jade Emperor in anger banished her to live as a mortal on Earth. She could return to Heaven he said if she contributed valuable service during her time on Earth.

Ch'ang-O as a mortal was a daughter of poor farming family. When she 18 years old she met the young archer Houyi and they became close friends. One day something strange happened. Ten suns rose over the Earth in the sky instead of one and began to burn the Earth. As an expert archer, Houyi saw the suns and was able to shoot down nine suns and leave one with his bow and arrow. Houyi was a hero for saving the Earth. He became king of the land and married Ch'ang-O.

In time Houyi became more of a demanding ruler. He ordered an elixir be made to give him immortality. The pill for this elixir was almost ready for him when Ch'ang-O discovered it and swallowed the pill. Houyi found this out that he went after Ch'ang-O in anger. She escaped out of a window in the palace but did not fall out. She floated instead up into the sky because of the pill's effects. She landed on the moon. The king still tried to shoot her down with arrows but with no success due to her immortality.

Ch'ang-O felt lonely at first on the moon but then befriended the Jade Rabbit show also lives on the moon and makes herbal medicine and mixes elixirs. Houyi eventually ascended to live and build a palace on the sun and so Ch'ang-O and Houyi came to symbolize yin and yang.

The Mid-Autumn Festival also called the Moon Festival in China happens on the 15th day of the 8th month in the Chinese lunar calendar which is sometime in late September or early October around the Autumn Equinox. It is an autumn harvest festival and one of the most important celebrations of the year in China. This festival is also celebrated in Chinese communities everywhere including Chinatown in New York and San Francisco.

The moon is fullest and brightest this day of year and is called the Harvest Moon. The Chinese relied the lunar cycles and phases for planting and harvesting so this Mi-Autumn Festival is to celebrate the end of autumn harvest and to bring friends and family together to give thanks to the Earth.

Ch'ang-O is worshipped as the Moon Goddess on this day. An altar is set up facing the full moon to her outdoors and in homes and gardens. Photos of Ch'ang-O floating up to the moon as well as on the moon with the Jade Rabbit are also sold for this festival and decorate homes. This day is also considered Ch'ang-O's birthday. On this day she inspires devotion in all relationships and sends energy for growth and manifestation in all life areas. This is a time for women to ask the moon goddess Ch'ang-O to bless them with good fortune for the coming year. When the moon rises women light incense and offer thirteen pastries to Ch'ang-O called moon cakes shaped like the moon as a symbol for the cycle of the year. They light candles, bow, and pray to her. They then recite poems in her honor. Girls of the family stay up late to pray their mothers have long and happy lives. Stories of Ch'ang-O are told this night. At midnight everyone honors Ch'ango and Jade Rabbit and eat the moon cakes under the full moon.

A feast is made for this festival that symbolize the moon including dumplings shaped like crescent moons, moon shaped rice cakes, melons, grapes, cookies, and moon cakes are some traditional foods. Families and friends gather on the night of the Mid-Autumn festival and enjoy this feast under the full moon. On the way to this feast they carry brightly lit lanterns that symbolize the moon light shaped as various animals, birds, or fish in procession outside for the celebration at night. This is a time for family reunions. Planting Mid-Autumn trees is also a traditional activity for this day and Fire Dragon Dances.

Ch'ang-O is associated with courage, power , and fertility. You can call upon her for courage and to break free, growth, manifestation, to believe in oneself, and a fresh start.

Ch'ang-O Ritual Belief in Oneself

SUPPLIES
1 White Candles
1 Silver Candle
Incense
Oil to anoint candle
Moonstone
Altar cloth-silver, dark blue, or black
Small round bowl of water
Lunar Journal

SET UP ALTAR.

Place the white candle in the Center, the silver candle in the South, the moonstone in the North, the incense in the East, and the bowl of water in the West. These represent the five directions and elements. Place the journal and any other symbols, images, or food offerings as well on the altar.

Anoint candles with oil and light them.
Light incense and purify space.

Cast the circle using the five directions and elements:
North Elements of Earth
East Element of Air
South Element of Fire
West Element of Water
Center Element of Spirit and the Goddess

INVOCATION:

"Ch'ang-O, Moon Goddess Guide me to manifest the goals, wishes, and intentions in my life I am setting now."

Meditate visualizing what you would like to create and manifest in your life right now.

After this is clear write down those specific intentions, goals, and wishes you would like to set now.

Say "Ch'ang-O bless me with the belief in myself and courage to take the steps to manifest these intentions, goals, and wishes I am setting now "

The circle is open but unbroken.

Let the candles burn out and begin to work on manifesting what you have written on your list in your Lunar Journal.

Ix Chel

Ix Chel (pronounced EE-SHELL) is the Mayan moon goddess. She is the mystery and joy of our female sexuality, mother of earth and all life, patroness of the healing arts, weaving, childbirth, and destiny. She is sometimes called "Lady Rainbow" and is often pictured as a serpent crone wearing a skirt and crossbones. She carries an upside-down vessel in her hands which represents the nourishing gift of water, our most essential life-giving element. She wears a serpent on her head representing her transformation from the winter to spring energy – shedding her winter skin in order to blossom anew into spring to a fresh stage in the life cycle.

Goddess Ix Chel was almost too beautiful, this girl with opalescent skin, who sat in the skies brushing her shimmering hair for hours on end. All the gods were captivated by her. That is, all but one. Kinich Ahau, the Sun God, seemed immune to Ix Chel's charms. Yet he was the only one she really ever wanted. For years she had longed for him as she watched him glide across the sky in all his golden splendor. But the more Ix Chel followed him around, the worse the weather on earth became. As she chased after him the tides would rise, creating floods that inundated the fields and caused the crops to die. So enamored was she, that Ix Chel did not even notice the havoc she was causing.

Ix Chel bore the Sun God four sons. They were the jaguar gods and could creep through the night unseen.

They were named for the four directions and each one was responsible for holding up his corner of the sky.

Unfortunately, Ix Chel's love affair with the Sun God drew the ire of her disapproving grandfather. In his anger he struck Ix Chel with lightning, killing her. For the next 183 days she lay lifeless as hundreds of dragonflies surrounded her body and sang to her. Waking suddenly, she returned to the palace of the Sun God.

Their relationship was turbulent. Kinich Ahau had a suspicious nature and was often consumed with jealousy. To make matters worse, he also had a fiery temper. Suspecting that the innocent Ix Chel was having an affair with his brother (the Morning Star), Kinich Ahay threw her out of the sky. She quickly found refuge with the vulture gods. Hearing this, Kinich Ahau rushed to plead with her to return and promised never to treat her so poorly again. Little time passed before he became jealous and abusive again.

Finally, Ix Chel realized he was not going to change. She decided to leave him for good. Waiting until he fell asleep, she crept out into the night, taking the form of a jaguar and becoming invisible whenever he came searching for her. Many nights she spent on her sacred island (Cozumel) nursing women during their pregnancies and childbirth.

Ix Chel, like other moon goddesses, governed women's reproductive systems so it was quite understandable that she would become the protector of women during pregnancy and labor. The small Isla Mujeres (Isle of Women) was devoted to the worship of Ix Chel. Comfortable with all phases of life, she was honored as the weaver of the life cycle. She protected the fertility of women and was also the keeper of the souls of the dead.

She is a shape-shifter, consorting with the rabbit in spring (fertility and life-giving abundance). She is at once a maiden (goddess of fertility and life), a mother (protector of women in childbirth) and a crone. The serpent reflects her status as a wise woman dispensing healing visions. She is the keeper of the life cycle, goddess of all new life and keeper of the bones and souls of the dead.

Wife to the high god Izamna, she oversees weaving, medicine, and childbirth. Like the First Mother, she is a moon goddess who is depicted sitting in a moon sign holding a rabbit. Ix Chel is a complex Goddess of ancient Mexico. She was worshipped by the Putun and Yucatec Maya. The hare was one of Her primary symbols.

In Maya myths She was the angry old woman who emptied the vials of her wrath on the earth, and assisted the serpent in creating the deluge. Ix Chel was the goddess of floods and cloud bursts, a malevolent deity likely to cause sudden destruction in a tropical storm. She was the consort of Itzamna and appears as a clawed water goddess, surrounded by the symbols of death and destruction, a writhing serpent on her head and crossbones embroidered on her skirt.

As an ancient fertility goddess, Ix Chel was responsible for sending rain to nourish the crops. When fulfilling that function she was called "Lady Rainbow". She helped ensure fertility by overturning her sacred womb jar so that the waters would flow.

Though sometimes depicted as a goddess of catastrophe (the woman who stands by as the world floods) many of her myths show her in a more benevolent light – as a goddess who refused to become a victim of oppression. This was a woman who when faced with adversity took charge of her life and turned it around!

Ix Chel encourages us to acknowledge the negative forces affecting our lives. And she prompts us to assert ourselves fully in the face of physical or emotional violence that would diminish our sense of self. She is all of life's fertility and is the continuation of all life. She is the mystery and joy of female sexuality and protector of our children. She is a healer, the Goddess of Medicine, who knows all of the healing gifts of the

Earth and Her children, the plants. Her flower is the marigold. Her methods of teaching and healing are by example as She comforts those who are ill or in pain. She is the energy of all water, our most essential life-giving ingredient. Nourishing rains and crystal clear rivers are Her gifts. As the tree of life, milk pours from Her breasts just as blood pours from her womb.

They Mayan stepped pyramid is Ix Chel's mountain where She reigns as the feathered serpent energy of transformation. Her totem is the snake which sheds its skin and is continually reborn. Her lap is the red jaguar throne of authority and power. She is often shown with a rabbit which symbolizes Her life-giving abundance and fertility. She is the young Maiden ripe with flowering life as well as the old crone of wisdom, pouring the waters of life from Her cauldron.

She is viewed as creative inspiration for artists and crafts people. She weaves the web of life and is the matron of weavers and those who make clothing. The moon is Her symbol and as She moves through the cycles of waxing, full, waning and darkness She mirror's the mysteries of our bodies and our blood cycles.

Moonlight Manifestations to Ixchell

IxChel is a versatile Goddess, and one I have great devotion to. The following rituals align with the moon phases to help you connect with Ixchel's different aspects and bring her energy into your life.

(Remember when speaking her name out loud that it is pronounced "ee-shell.")

You can do these mini-rituals for the cycle of one moon or any time they are needed.

New Moon Manifestation

Think ahead ~ what aspect of your life do you want to be healed at this time?

Preparation ~ create a sacred space near water (river, bathtub, shower, pond, ocean) that is quiet and safe, where you won't be interrupted. Decorate with the color black, and prepare a black candle. Bring an item that represents what you are healing. Bring an offering for Ixchel.

Light your black candle. Then call to Ixchel out loud: "Ixchel, I honor and celebrate you. Please accept this offering as a token of my humbleness and awe of your magnificence and power."

Enter into the water. "Oh Great Goddess, Crone, Destroyer, Goddess of Waters and Rainstorms. Ixchel with your mighty bucket of water, destroy that which is no longer healthy, cleanse me inside and out, and wash it all away. I honor and release <what you are healing> - it is yours now Great Goddess Ixchel."

Sit in meditation with the energy of Ixchel and be open to any messages or guidance that she has to offer you. Burn the black candle all the way to remind you to submit to healing on all levels.

WAXING MOON MANIFESTATION

Preparation ~ create a sacred space that is quiet and safe, where you won't be interrupted. Bring creative projects that you are planning or working on. Decorate with the color orange, and prepare an orange candle. Bring an offering for Ixchel.

Light your orange candle. Then call to Ixchel out loud: "Ixchel, I honor and celebrate you. Please accept this offering as a token of my humbleness and awe of your magnificence and power."

"Oh Great Goddess of Weavers and Artisans, Ixchel imbue me with creativity and joy in the work that I undertake. Bless <this project> that it may be successful and beautiful."

Sit in meditation with the energy of Ixchel and be open to any messages or guidance that she has to offer you. Keep the orange candle to light and rekindle the creative fire if you find it runs low at some other time.

FULL MOON MANIFESTATION

Think ahead ~ do you want blessings for fertility, pregnancy and childbirth? For fertility in creative endeavors? For abundance in your life?

Preparation ~ create a sacred space that is quiet and safe, where you won't be interrupted. Decorate your space with rabbits, with the color white, and prepare a white candle. Bring an offering for Ixchel.

Light your white candle. Then call to Ixchel out loud: "Ixchel, I honor and celebrate you. Please accept this offering as a token of my humbleness and awe of your magnificence and power."

"Oh Great Earth Goddess, Protector of Women and Children, Goddess of New Life, Ixchel imbue my life with abundance in spirit, body and mind. Bless <my intentions> that they may be fertile, and prosperous. Protect them and aid them on their way to manifestation.?

Sit in meditation with the energy of Ixchel and be open to any messages or guidance that she has to offer you. Keep the white candle to light and use it to invoke her protection or fertile energy if you need it again some other time.

Waning Moon Manifestation

Preparation ~ create a sacred space that is quiet and safe, where you won't be interrupted. Decorate with the color red, snakes, and prepare a red candle. Bring an offering for Ixchel.

Light your red candle. Then call to Ixchel out loud: "Ixchel, I honor and celebrate you. Please accept this offering as a token of my humbleness and awe of your magnificence and power."

"Oh Great Goddess of Women's Sexuality, Keeper of the Cycles of Life and Death, teach me your medicine and magic. Teach me your wisdom and teach me your power."

Sit in meditation with the energy of Ixchel and be open to any messages or guidance that she has to offer you. Keep the red candle to light and reconnect to your inner medicine and magic at some other time if you need it.

Dark Moon Manifestation I

Preparation ~ create a sacred space that is quiet and safe, where you won't be interrupted. Decorate with the color black, and prepare a black candle. Bring items that represent those who have crossed over. Bring an offering for Ixchel.

Light your black candle. Then call to Ixchel out loud: "Ixchel, I honor and celebrate you. Please accept this offering as a token of my humbleness and awe of your magnificence and power."

"Oh Great Goddess, Keeper of the Bones and the Dead, watch over my beloved <person> and show them the way if they get lost. Teach me wisdom in the midst of my grief and pain."

Sit in meditation with the energy of Ixchel and be open to any messages or guidance that she has to offer you. Keep the black candle to light again if you need to revisit your grief or loved ones.

The Charge of the Goddess

Fewer poems have had the kind of effect on people like the Charge of the Goddess. An inspirational text that is usually spoken after the ritual Drawing Down the Moon, The Charge is the promise of the Goddess to all her seekers, that she will teach and guide them.

Parts of the text originated with Charles Godfrey Leland's 1899 book Aradia, that introduces the concept, which was further cultivated by Doreen Valiente adding some phrases adapted from The Book of the Law and The Gnostic Mass by Aleister Crowley in the 1940s.

However it is Starhawk's adaptation that seems to speak most to people. Her version added the Charge of the Star Goddess and invited the night sky, the Moon, and more. First published in 1979 in the seminal work, The Spiral Dance, it is reproduced here with blessing from Starhawk.

CHARGE OF THE GODDESS
Traditional by Doreen Valiente, as adapted by Starhawk

Listen to the words of the Great Mother, Who of old was called Artemis, Astarte, Dione, Melusine, Aphrodite, Cerridwen, Diana, Arionrhod, Brigid, and by many other names:

Whenever you have need of anything, once a month, and better it be when the moon is full, you shall assemble in some secret place and adore the spirit of Me Who is Queen of all the Wise.

You shall be free from slavery, and as a sign that you be free you shall be naked in your rites.

Sing, feast, dance, make music and love, all in My Presence, for Mine is the ecstasy of the spirit and Mine also is joy on earth.

For My law is love is unto all beings. Mine is the secret that opens the door of youth, and Mine is the cup of wine of life that is the cauldron of Cerridwen, that is the holy grail of immortality.

I give the knowledge of the spirit eternal, and beyond death I give peace and freedom and reunion with those that have gone before.

Nor do I demand aught of sacrifice, for behold, I am the Mother of all things and My love is poured out upon the earth.

Hear the words of the Star Goddess, the dust of Whose feet are the hosts of Heaven, whose body encircles the universe:

I Who am the beauty of the green earth and the white moon among the stars and the mysteries of the waters,

I call upon your soul to arise and come unto me. For I am the soul of nature that gives life to the universe.

From Me all things proceed and unto Me they must return.

Let My worship be in the heart that rejoices, for behold, all acts of love and pleasure are My rituals.

Let there be beauty and strength, power and compassion, honor and humility, mirth and reverence within you.

And you who seek to know Me, know that the seeking and yearning will avail you not, unless you know the Mystery: for if that which you seek, you find not within yourself, you will never find it without.

For behold, I have been with you from the beginning, and I am That which is attained at the end of desire.

Lunar Journal
Inviting the Goddess

- Light with the intention of creating a space of sacredness.

- Spend a few moments in contemplation, recalling the symbology of the Triple Moon Goddess. Because the psyche responds to symbols and images far more readily than to words, I often find that invoking this archetypal imagery can open up realms of the personal unconscious that are otherwise unavailable.

- With a notebook and pen close by, close your eyes and summon Goddess inwardly. Ask that the Goddess energy in you be present. Say, "Let me speak to the Goddess"

- At this point, drop inside and notice what is invoked in you by this request. Let yourself feel the energy of the Goddess within you. If it feels natural, you might even begin to speak out loud as Goddess. How would Goddess speak? What would she say to you? Or you can go directly to the next step.

- With your dominant hand, write, "Who are you?" or "Tell me about yourself." Then take the pen in your other hand and write an answer.

- With your dominant hand, write, "What do you want to express?" With the non dominant hand, write your answer.

- Continue the dialogue as long as it has energy. You can always come back to it later.

- When the dialogue feels finished, sit quietly for a few moments, being present with the breath. Notice the spaces between the in-breath and the out-breath, the out-breath and the in-breath. Without holding your breath, see if you can be aware of how the breath arises and subsides from stillness. This open space is the essential nature of the Goddess energy.

- Thank your inner Goddess. Place the picture or image of Moon where you can see it every day.

- Take an action that feels connected to the energy you've accessed. Goddess like activities might include wild dancing or kicking, speaking a truth you have been afraid to voice, asserting a preference, doing something you never did before.

- Note any dreams, insights, or shifts that arise in the next few days.

Blue Moon
Deep Wisdom

We may learn wisdom
first, by reflection.
Which is noblest
  — Confucius

    Of all the moons we have encountered, most of you will be familiar with the name "Blue Moon." Between, "once in a blue moon" and the song lyrics, "blue moon, I saw you standing alone" this moon has become common in our vernacular. But the Blue Moon isn't *that* rare, and never stands alone. In fact this phenomenon we call Blue Moon, occurs when two full Moons happen in one calendar month, hence not alone.

    Since the phase period of the Moon is 29.5 days, you usually only have one full Moon each month. But each month it's a little earlier than the previous month and eventually you'll find 2 full Moons in a single month. This occurs about every 2.5 years, and the second full Moon is called the "blue Moon".

There is no physical difference in appearance, the second full Moon looks like a regular full Moon.

According to folklorists, the term "Blue Moon" is at least 400 years old. The earliest known references to a blue Moon were intended as examples of improbable events or something that could never happen. As time passed the expression evolved to mean something that rarely or never happened. Hence the expression "Once in a Blue Moon" which is still popular today.

I modern communities, he origins of the meaning of a Blue Moon vary. And the legend or origin of these meanings cannot be substantiated. However, some believe the second full Moon holds the knowledge of the Grandmother Goddess (or the Crone) and therefore contains the wisdom of the 3-fold the energy. This can be associated with the Goddess in her 3 forms of Maiden, Mother, Crone. It can also be associated with the 3 natures of self as Mind, Body, Spirit.

In other traditions traditions the phases of the Moon represent the transition of knowledge within the Goddess. The quarter Moons representing the Maiden Goddess, the New Moon the Mother Goddess, the Full Moon the Grand Mother Goddess (which maybe one reason we refer to the Moon as "Grandmother Moon". The Blue Moon then is seen as the transition of the Grandmother or Crone to the Divine level of existence.

She becomes an expression of evolution of wisdom, as well as an example of the circle of life.

Another view is that the Blue Moon represents a time of heightened or clearer communication between our physical being and the Divine. Often the energy of the Divine is seen in the form of the Grandmother Goddess or the Crone Goddess. It can also be viewed as a link between the physical and the spiritual making communication with spirit easier and more apt to yield insightful and enlightened communications.

The Blue Moon is the perfect time to seek wisdom, knowledge and understanding. Yet we needn't wait for just the Blue Moon, as The Charge of the Goddess said, any time you have need of me, and better when the Moon is Full..." Turn to aligning your energies and cultivating your wisdom fearlessly.

There is an expression, where shall wisdom be found? Just by reading this book, you are seeking wisdom. Seeking divine knowing and healing that inspires and nurtures the soul. Wisdom is not something instantly attained, it takes years to cultivate and become Grandmother Moon. But that aspect of self is always a part of us. Steadfast and true! Let us seeking wisdom and knowing.

Wisdom Manifestation

This is a manifestation and intention building exercise to help bring wisdom to yourself or another.

Supplies
1 Red Candle
1 White Candle

Manifestation:
Start clearing you mind of all thoughts. Clearing your ritual space of all negative energy cast a Circle as done in previous rituals.

Bless candles with any oils or moon waters!

Say a short blessing for guidance such as"
Grandmother Moon under the stars tonight, fill me with wisdom and second sight. Lead me to my highest potential and fill me with manifest potential.

Light the Red Candle Saying Your Name:
In love and light I send you/myself wisdom on this night, Wisdom to know what things to change, wisdom to this system rearrange. Fir make this wisdom strong, burn so that it may last long.

Light the White Candle Saying: White Candle pure and bright in purity I do this magic tonight. May this magic have no reverse and on no one a curse.

Lunar Journal: Wisdom Shall Be Found?

We see the moon in the sky, radiant and know that it is there. In this book I have tried to present both the science and the lore. But how do we know the difference between knowing something is true and just wishful thinking? Here are some guiding questions to help you come into knowing?

Think about some things you were taught as a child but maybe turned out not to be true? How did it feel to come into a wisdom different than what you previously thought?

If you could lean into one piece of wisdom about the Moon from this book, what might that be? How might you go about knowing more? The end of this book provides resources for more wisdom!

viii
MOON TIDES
FLOWING WITH GRAVITY

*"Summer ends, and Autumn comes,
and he who would have it otherwise
would have high tide always
and a full moon every night."*
— Hal Borland

No book about the Moon would be complete without some mention of the tides. To be fair, not every person reading this will have access to Oceanic waters. Yet, what I present here is not so much science as it is lore. Regardless of whether there is an ocean in your back yard, the way the Moon interacts with water effects everything!

The moon's relationship with water was of particular interest to the ancient people. Our Ancestors observed how the moon affected the tides and how it reflected upon the waters, shimmering and bright. For each moon phase, season and hour there is an associated tide. Tides are created because the Earth and the Moon are attracted to one another other by a magnetic pull, and since water is a fluid, the gravity of the Earth cannot hold it still and therefore the water flows in harmony with the movements of the Moon. As the Earth moves and the Moon pulls, the ocean is constantly moving from high tide to low tide, with about twelve hours between two high tides.

The Sun also omits a gravitational pull, although its force is much less powerful. However, when both Moon and Sun are combined (i.e. on New and Full Moons) the gravitational pull is more and this is called a Spring Tide (note, this has nothing to do with the season of spring). This causes tidal variations such as very high tides and very low tides. When the Sun and Moon are not working together, the gravitational pull is less and the tides are not as extreme. These are called Neap Tides.

We use the tides by taking advantage of the natural energy flow available to them. Just like the tides of the sea, it is easier to go with the natural flow than against it, so taking notice of tide times and biorhythms of the planet can make ritual, intention setting, and manifestation work much more successful.

For instance, a Full Moon usually indicates that energy is at its peak. However if we also work at a High Tide during that Full Moon, then the results will be even more effective. Additionally, if we were working to banish, using a New Moon at Low Tide would be the best time for that particular manifestation.

You can usually find out about your local tides by checking the Shipping Forecasts and Tide Tables, which are easy to get hold of on the internet and are usually updated every day. With this, we can attribute a tide to each season of the year and parts of nature. These are called the Elemental Tides.

EARTH TIDE:
Begins at December's Full Moon
Peaks at February's Full Moon
Ends at March's Full Moon

FIRE TIDE:
Begins at April's Full Moon
Peaks at May's Full Moon
Ends at June's Full Moon

AIR TIDE:
Begins at July's Full Moon
Peaks at August's Full Moon
Ends at September's Full Moon

WATER TIDE:
Begins at October's Full Moon
Peaks at November's Full Moon
Ends at December's Full Moon

The Elemental tides allow us to use the power of the tides together with the Wheel of the Year, and our journey through own lives. The tides of Earth relate to matters of the body, tides of Fire relate to matters of the spirit, tides of Air relate to matters of the mind and the tides of Water relate to matters of the emotions.

So for instance, to hold a rite in August on a Full Moon and at a High Tide, is sure to be the most effective time to work towards your mental abilities or studying. And a ritual held at December on a New Moon and at a Low Tide, is likely to be a most effective time of working towards releasing ties to an old relationship and making way for the new.

OCEANIC BREATHING

Ujjayi (pronounced oo-jai) is an ancient yogic breathing technique that helps calm the mind and body. The world translates into 'victorious breath' however the hissing sound made, often reminds people of the ocean. Ujjayi has a balancing influence on the entire body, particularly the respiratory system, and releases feelings of irritation and frustration.

With all breath work, knowing your body is the first step towards wholeness. I recommend trying this breath work first on the full and new moons.

Here is how to perform Ujjayi breath:
Take an inhalation that is slightly deeper than normal. With your mouth closed, exhale through your nose while constricting your throat muscles. If you are doing this correctly, you should sound like Darth Vader from Star Wars.

Another way to get the hang of this practice is to try exhaling the sound "haaaaah" with your mouth open. Now make a similar sound with your mouth closed, feeling the outflow of air through your nasal passages. Once you have mastered this on the outflow, use the same method for the inflow breath, gently constricting your throat as you inhale.

Try shifting into Ujjayi breath whenever you find yourself becoming aggravated or stressed, and you should notice a prompt soothing effect. Ujjayi breathing will help you stay focused and centered as you flow from one life situation to another..

Healing Waters

Fill a bathtub with water of a temperature that feels right to you. Place a glass of clean drinking water nearby in case you get thirsty. You might want to light a beeswax or soya candle and turn off the lights. (I find turning off the bathroom lights to be an enhancement, possibly because any artificial light changes the energy of the room.)

Before stepping into the filled tub, ask Water to cleanse, heal, and purify the deepest pain inside of you, whether it be physical, mental, or emotional. Your active participation in asking for healing is very important. When I ask for a healing from Water, I sense welcoming and healing love enveloping me as I step into the tub; it almost feels as if the water reaches out to take care of me.

Once settled and soaking, breathe slowly and deeply. Ask for a message about your pain. Its source will usually be identified almost immediately, and more information may be provided about how to help enhance the healing, such as singing or reciting a mantra.

I've had some profound spiritual healing with this water meditation. For example, I've been given the insight about why some relationships affect me the way they do and how to heal the part of me that is vulnerable. Even if you don't sense a message during your bath, you will always sense and feel the healing results soon after and throughout the day. Just be a witness -- in a meditative way -- during the bath, so you can just "be" and receive. Let yourself feel free to go with the flow.

After about 20 minutes, thank the Waters that reside within you. Also, express thanks to the waters of the tub for the healing, and then step out of the tub. Saying "thank you" for water's healing upon entering and during the bath is helpful too, because the energy of gratitude is healing in its own right and will help elevate the vibration of the water in the tub and in your body.

HEALING SOAK RECIPE

1 cup of epsom salt or sea salt
4 drops of lavender oil for soothing aches
or
4 drops of eucalyptus essential oil to open breathing
2 tea bags of Chamomile Tea (it's cheap and it works!)

Place all into tub and bless waters.
Powers of the Moon so Full
Heal me to a state that's true

Lunar Journal: Breathing the Tides

As I mention, not every person who uses this book will have access to oceanic bodies of water. However that doesn't mean that we can't draw upon the timing of the tides to manifest greatness.

After taking a healing bath, ask yourself what you released down the drain? What things did you notice while soaking? Did you feel anything different in your body?

Healing waters are a time of great introspection. align yourself with a moon phase and invite the mysteries!

viii
THE MANY MOONS
12 Full Moon Faces

" May the Moon carry your sadness away,
may the flowers fill your heart with beauty,
may hope forever wipe away your tears,
and, above all, may silence make you strong."
~ Chief Dan George

Many human cultures have given names to the full Moon throughout the year. Different full Moon names can be found among the Chinese, Celtic, Old English, and New Guinea cultures, to name a few. In addition, Native American tribes often used Moon phases and cycles to keep track of the seasons and gave a unique name to each recurring full Moon. The full Moon names were used to identify the entire month during which each occurred.

Although many Native American Tribes gave distinct names to the full Moon, the most well known names of the full Moon come from the Algonquin tribes who lived in the area of New England and westward to Lake Superior. The Algonquin tribes had perhaps the greatest effect on the early European settlers in America, and the settlers adopted the Native American habit of naming the Moons. They even invented some of their own names that have been passed down through time.

The names given here aren't the only ones that have been used. Every full Moon, with one exception, had variations on its name among various Algonquin tribes, not to mention other tribes throughout North America. But the names below are the most common. Some of the variations are also mentioned.

Lunar Journal:
Inviting the Monthly Moon

Each month welcomes a new theme to deepen the bond we share with the Moon. Take a moment to reflect what the Algonquin's might be observed in life. This is a time for deep listening, and transformations. Each month invites the opportunity to know ourselves better through a ritual and Lunar Journal theme.

January: The Wolf Moon

In January snow gathers deep in the woods and the howling of wolves can be heard echoing in the cold still air.

Lunar Journal:
The year is cycling anew! Instead of an intention, how about a manifestation. What are you looking to develop from a negative to a positive?

Lunar Magic

On the full Moon, light altar candles. Hold the unlit black candle in your hands and say: "This holds me back. No more will it control me. No more is it a part of me."

Place the black candle on your altar and hold the unlit white candle in your hands. Say: "This is my might and my courage and my victory. This battle is already won."

Place the white candle next to the black one on your altar. Light the black candle and picture the bad habit you want to break. Light the white candle and picture yourself free from your bad habit. After a few moments of imagining victory, put out the black candle, then the white. Repeat a week later if necessary.

February: The Hunger Moon

Snow piles even higher in February, giving this Moon its most common name due to the challenging hunting conditions.

Lunar Journal:

What are you hungry for? This is a time of deep introspection and sometimes we need a sign to guide us! Soon we will plant seeds for spring.

Lunar Magic

Light the candle, let it burn while you chant:

"From this to you I send a sign,
Letting you know what's on my mind,
Bring the answer unto thee,
Needing to know what the truth could be."

March: The Crust Moon

Snow slowly begins to melt, the ground softens with the formation of crusts on the snow from repeated thawing and freezing. Christian settlers also called this the Lenten Moon and considered it the last Moon of winter.

Lunar Journal:

As we melt away the layers and prepare for warmth, what layers are you willing to shed?

Lunar Magic

Begin by taking the silver candle in hand and start to send silver calming and emotional energy in to the candle. As you do this chant the following 7 times;

"Silver power, silver light
Melt away my layers on this night.
Candle of the Moon, candle of the stars
Restore my emotions and heal my scars.
Candle of paraffin, candles of wax
Invite me with warmth, this I ask."

Now place the candle and place it on your altar and light it. Feel its energy resonate out all about you. Consider doing this nightly during the Crust Moon.

April: The Pink Moon

Flowers begin to appear, including the widespread grass pink or wild ground phlox this indicates welcoming signs of full spring.

Lunar Journal:

It is time to plant some springtime intentions that will manifest into Summer. What is the beauty and abundance you wish to receive?

Lunar Magic

Arrange on your sacred space a clear glass bowl with a small mirror in the bottom of the bowl. Add water, and place three white floating candles in the dish. Gaze into the mirror and meditate on the reflected candlelight.

"As the Moon controls the tides of the sea,
So it's rhythm rules our living lives.
Through cycles that are ever changing,
first Waxing and then Waning,
In different phases, yet the same.
What was once poor, lacking and desilute,
Now bring forth abundance for _____."

May: The Flower Moon

Flowers come into full bloom and corn is ready to plant. Also called the Corn Planting Moon and the Milk Moon.

Lunar Journal:

Time to head outside. On a Moonlit night, find your favorite spot to relax and spend some time soaking in the Moon's beams. Let us plant some seeds?

Lunar Magic

Stand near your favorite spot, under the Moon beams and say this :

*"This world is a place of many a birth,
so give me the power of mother earth.
I plant the seeds of new beginnings
and welcome forth the great willings"*

Invite this blessings during the Waxing Moon phase.

June: The Strawberry Moon

Strawberry-picking season reaches its peak during this time. This is one of the few names that was universal to all Algonquin tribes.

Lunar Journal:

Strawberries are a sweet reward after a long winter. How might you reward yourself for your work? What brings you bliss

Lunar Magic

This isn't so much lunar magic as an invitation with a magical result. Gather some berries in season. With these delightful fruits, let yourself come into a mindful awareness of abundance.

As you begin to eat, invite the texture of the fruit. Eating slowly and with intention, what does it taste like, what are the textures? Are they different than you have experienced in the past? How might you welcome the difference in sensation you feel into other areas of your life?

July: The Thunder Moon

With the intense heat of summer, the Moon becomes the Thunder Moon in July. Frequent thunderstorms join the Moon to illumine the sky.

Lunar Journal:

Summer invites rain that nurtures the often parched earth. With it comes often powerful thunder and dazzling lightening. When you nurture your soul, how does it make you more powerful and dazzling like lightening?

Lunar Magic

Invite the summertime with this Say this manifestation outside in a chalk drawn circle, and let the warm summer rain wash away bringing you powerful cleansing and dazzling radiance.

> "Bring the rain down,
> giving life to the ground,
> Energy to feed the seed,
> Lunar gifts unto me.
> Hear the thunder,
> And see it's wonder,
> Dazzling and bright
> In the pale Moonlight."

August: The Red Moon

The reddish appearance of the Moon through the frequent sultry hazes of August also prompted a few tribes to dub it the Red Moon. Other names included the Green Corn Moon and the Grain Moon.

Lunar Journal:

What are you hungry for? This is a time of deep introspection and sometimes we need a sign to guide us!. Soon we will plant seeds for spring.

Lunar Magic

Light the candle, let it burn while you chant:

"From this to you I send a sign,
Letting you know what's on my mind,
Bring the answer unto thee,
Needing to know what the truth could be."

September: The Harvest Moon

Many of the Native American tribes' staple foods, such as corn, pumpkins, squash, beans, and rice, are ready for gathering at this time. The strong light of the Harvest Moon allowed European farmers to work late into the night to harvest their crops. The Harvest Moon does not always occur in September. Traditionally, the name goes to the full Moon closest to the autumn equinox, which falls during October once or twice a decade. Sometimes the September full Moon was called the Corn Moon.

Lunar Journal:

What are you hungry for? This is a time of deep introspection and sometimes we need a sign to guide us! Soon we will plant seeds for spring.

Lunar Magic

Light the candle, let it burn while you chant:

"From this to you I send a sign,
Letting you know what's on my mind,
Bring the answer unto thee,
Needing to know what the truth could be."

OCTOBER: THE HUNTER'S MOON

After the fields have been reaped, the leaves begin to fall and the deer are fat and ready for eating. Hunters can ride easily over the fields' stubble, and the fox and other animals are more easily spotted. Some years the Harvest Moon falls in October instead of September.

Lunar Journal:

What are you hungry for? This is a time of deep introspection and sometimes we need a sign to guide us! Soon we will plant seeds for spring.

LUNAR MAGIC

Light the candle, let it burn while you chant:

"From this to you I send a sign,
Letting you know what's on my mind,
Bring the answer unto thee,
Needing to know what the truth could be."

November: The Beaver Moon

At this time of year the beavers are busy preparing for winter, and it's time to set beaver traps and secure a store of warm fur before the swamps freeze over. Some tribes called this the Frosty Moon.

Lunar Journal:

What are you hungry for? This is a time of deep introspection and sometimes we need a sign to guide us! Soon we will plant seeds for spring.

Lunar Magic

Light the candle, let it burn while you chant:

"From this to you I send a sign,
Letting you know what's on my mind,
Bring the answer unto thee,
Needing to know what the truth could be."

December: The Snow Moon

Winter takes a firm hold and temperatures plummet at this time. As the winter nights lengthen and the Moon spends more time above the horizon opposite a low sun. The full Moon name often used by Christian settlers is the "Moon before Yule".

Lunar Journal:

What are you hungry for? This is a time of deep introspection and sometimes we need a sign to guide us! Soon we will plant seeds for spring.

Lunar Magic

On the night of the Snow Moon, announce your magical intentions to the Snow Moon. As a token of thanks, light a violet candle and speak to her:

"As the Earth wears a cocoon of white,
In icy splendor Snow Moon, you guard the night.
Let me make changes, let me be reborn,
Now I plant the seed of magic; I can transformed."

Leave your candle lit until it goes out on its own.

HEALING MOON
Luna Curativa

"It is a beautiful and delightful sight to behold the body of the Moon."
— Galileo

For thousands of years, the very first forms of magic were healing magic. Healers used the energies and properties of our great Earth to bring the ailing back into a state of health and peace. While the Sun propagated the land with harvest, they observed that all living things responded to the Waxing and Waning of the Moon. During the Full Moon shellfish are plumper and more succulent, and mammals have more blood in their bodies and stronger heartbeats. Women tend to menstruate during the New Moon and ovulate during the Full Moon. The herbs used by ancient healers were said to be best when picked during a particular phase of the Moon.

I have found the Moon to be a powerful healing ally and have found using herbal therapies in harmony with the phases of the Moon to be a very powerful healing strategy. While, I am not an professional herbalist, I am drawn to herbal alchemy to help realign my body and soothe my soul. The Moon provides us with the tools to cultivate and awareness of the rhythms of nature in formulating the best self care.

WAXING MOON

The Waxing phase of the Moon is the best time to build the body up. This is when I use nurturing herbs and tonics to strengthen the body's natural immunities. Raspberry leaf is an excellent tonic for reproductive organs; hawthorn berries are good for the cardiovascular system; nettle is a great blood tonic; marshmallow root is a soothing tonic for the urinary tract; astragalas is a wonderful immune system tonic; burdock is a good liver tonic; red clover builds fertility; oat straw is good for the nervous system; and alfalfa is a fantastic all-around nutritive tonic.

These herbs are simple and gentle. They are best taken in a cup of tea, three to five times a day. During the Waxing phase, I also like to increase water intake to avoid water retention. The more water we ingest, the less water our bodies attempt to retain.

This is also a good time to apply medicinal salves and to take therapeutic baths. Most importantly, I work during the Waxing Moon to ensure that the body has all the nutritional support it needs. This is the body's building time, and it needs a good supply of minerals, vitamins, carbohydrates, lipids, and amino acids to be healthy. I would also not attempt to fast or to lose weight during the Waxing Moon.

Use energy healing techniques to strengthen and reconnect with the earth. Be careful to ground and center when healing so that you never use up your own life force energy. The universe if full of energy to use, and by tapping into it you will be able to help many more people than you could by using just your energy alone.

Full Moon

The Full Moon lasts about three days. It is a very intense phase. Many women still ovulate with the Full Moon. This is the time when I apply the most powerful herbs. I like to use cayenne capsules to treat infections of any kind. Goldenseal is a well-known herbal antibiotic. Echinacea and Lomatium are anti-viral. Dong quai, black cohosh and chasteberry are excellent herbs for female hormonal fluctuations.

Energy healing work during the Full Moon is very powerful. On the energetic level, it acts like a magnifying mirror. The strong lunar energy pulls everything out of hiding and reflects it back at us. This is often the time during an acute illness when people feel their worst. The Full Moon intensifies whatever else is going on. Often people aren't even aware that they're sick until the Full Moon hits.

This is also an excellent time for psychological therapy. Emotions seem closer to the surface than usual and social inhibitions melt away. Agendas that have been simmering under the surface tend to come out under the light of the Full Moon. This is a time to strengthen relationships and reaffirm bonds. Never underestimate the healing power of simply holding someone's hand and listening. This is not the time for isolation or introspection. The Full Moon draws all of life toward it. Even the solid ground rises several inches when the Full Moon passes overhead!

Waning Moon

The Waning Moon is the best time to employ therapeutic fasts. I avoid drastic fasting. There is usually no need to starve the body to heal it. However, I found it helpful to limit my intake to juices and soups for a few days during the Waning Moon, particularly when I was struggling with the flu. I like to use purifying herbs in moderation at this time. Sage, ginger, lemon, thyme, lavender, and peppermint are all cleansing the clearing herbs.

The Waning Moon is also a good time to do sweats and diaphoretic (sweat producing) baths. In addition, if I were trying to kick a habit, I would do it during the Waning phase. Full body massages help circulation and strengthen the eliminative systems. Use energy healing techniques to server unhealthy bonds and strengthen boundaries.

Dark Moon

The Dark Moon is as powerful in its own way as the Full Moon. It is a time for taking stock. It is a phase of hibernation, retreat, and contemplation. Avoid crowds and gatherings and seek a little time for yourself. Unless an illness is at a critical phase, I frequently cease all therapies for a day or so and allow the body to seek its own level. Rest is crucial during the New Moon. Simple foods and quiet times are powerful healers.

Many women menstruate with the Dark Moon. It is natural to want to curl up in bed with a good book and nice cup of chamomile tea. Stronger nervines (relaxing herbs) are skullcap, hops, catnip, oatstraw and valerian.

Invigorating Moon Tea

A perfect morning tea, delicious served hot or iced. This

tea awakens the senses without caffeine.
- 4 cups Raspberry Leaf
- 1/2 cup Mint Leaf
- 1/4 cup Stevia Leaf
- 1 cup Nettle Leaf

Mix and use 1 tablespoon to brew by the glass or 1 cup to brew by the gallon. Add more or less Stevia to taste. Enjoy!

Dreamy Moon Tea

Lavender is a favorite scent and essential oil but it is too strong to be used alone in a tea.
- 1/2 cup Mint Leaf
- 2 Tablespoons Dried Lavender
- 2 Tablespoons Stevia (optional)

Mix all and store in an air-tight container. Use 1-2 tsp per cup of water to make hot or iced tea.

Calming Moon Tea

For stomach aches or for those prone to digestive troubles, this tea is very calming. The recipe is also very easy:
- 2 teaspoons mint leaf
- 1/2 teaspoon fennel seeds
- Pinch of dried ginger (optional)

Pour 1 cup of boiling water over it, steep, covered for 5 minutes and consume.

X
MOON SIGNS
Astrological Alignment

*"When the Moon is in the seventh house
and Jupiter aligns with Mars
then peace will guide the planets
and love will steer the stars".*

— Hair: The Musical

Your Moon sign reveals your inner self. It can give insight into the way you handle your emotions and fears; it can also give insight into the way you love and feel. The Moon also governs your moods. Have you ever met someone with your same sun sign and found that person to be nothing like you? You probably have different Moon signs.

It's in times of significant stress that your Moon sign can truly reveal itself. During trying times, your actions are influenced by emotion and instinct, so the side of you that you normally keep hidden can suddenly come to the surface and conflict with your usual outward personality. This can make you feel crazy, like you aren't acting like yourself, but it's in these times that you might be more "yourself" than ever. Moon signs are governed by their astrological make-up in the cosmos and also the elements. What follows is a general overview into the astrological and elemental make up of Moon signs.

To determine your Moon sign, do a simple search online for "birth chart" on the internet. I promise, modern technology makes it easier than the complex algebra equation to discover by hand.

CALLING THE ELEMENTS

Air moves us,
Fire transforms us,
Water shapes us,
Earth heals us,
And the balance of the wheel goes round and round,
And the balance of the wheel goes round.

Elemental Signs

Fire Moon Signs

People with fire sign Moons are passionate, direct, forthright and full of energy. They say what they mean, and are generally open and honest in their romantic lives. Highly sexed and with quite volatile tempers, they do like to be the centre of attention, and generally need a partner who will admire them and be happy to let them take the spotlight. Two fire Moon signs together makes for a highly charged and hot, hot, hot relationship, but one which can quickly burnout. Fire and air have excellent Moon sign compatibility, so a couple with one fire and one air Moon sign will inspire one another, and often enjoy a long lasting and mutually appreciate relationship.

Fire and earth Moon signs are a much more difficult combination, with each partner feeling that the other doesn't understand them; this couple deals with emotions very differently and could struggle. Fire and water Moon signs together have the potential to go either way, either creating a very steamy and intense relationship, or a complete damp squib, depending entirely on other factors in this couple's astrological makeup.

Earth Moon Signs

An earth Moon sign brings emotional stability to any partnership. People with earth Moons are cautious, patient, calm and kind, and not easily given to tantrums or displays of emotion. Very sensual, loving and faithful, these earthy souls are looking for a relationship which lasts. Two earth signs together means that Moon sign compatibility is strong…but potentially stuck. Not the most exciting of relationships, two earth Moons will endure, but possibly without many thrills.

An earth sign and a water sign, on the other hand, is a natural match. Here, both partners will balance out one another's emotional natures, providing an all round package for great emotional health. Earth and air Moon sign compatibility can be a little strained, as neither partner really "gets" the other's way of relating, but with work they can come to a mutual understanding.

AIR MOON SIGNS

People with air Moon signs are intellectual, imaginative, and talkative, always communicating but not necessarily laying bare their souls. Air Moon signs can be a little emotionally aloof and afraid to explore the deeper realms of emotion. Surprisingly, though, air and water Moon sign compatibility is strong, even though the couple are at opposite ends of the emotional spectrum – probably because both air and water Moons can be in love with love itself.

Air and fire Moon sign compatibility, as mentioned above, is very strong indeed, since fire needs air in order to thrive, whereas an earth Moon sign tends to weigh down the light and breezy emotions of an air Moon sign. When a couple with two Moon signs gets together, the relationship will be very chatty, lively and a lot of fun, but it could be missing that vital spark of passion.

Water Moon Signs

When the Moon is in a water sign, it shines very strongly indeed in the birth chart, because this is its natural home. Water Moon signs are emotional, highly intuitive and creative; easily moved both to tears and to laughter. This is heart on sleeve territory, with emotions visible to all. Water and fire Moon sign compatibility can be tremendously exciting, especially sexually, but ultimately, of course, water does put out fire. With an air sign Moon partner, the water Moon sign person will feel at ease and romantic, but dealing with the nitty gritty of life could be tough. Two water sign Moons together will drift in a sea of absolute sentimentality and romance, but drift is the operative word, and this partnership may never make it to safer shores.

Water and earth Moon sign compatibility is usually very strong, however – these two elements go together in the real world, and they go together exceptionally well in astrological compatibility too.

Lunar Journal:
Earth, Fire, Air, and Water.

Take moment to reflect back on your journey with the Moon, have you noticed times when you have felt different? Maybe it was the weather? A Full Moon time that there was excessive rain or intense heat?

Consider the elements; and how they might relate to how you can partner them with the Moon to manifest desires.

Zodiac Moon Alignments

Moon in Capricorn

The Capricorn Moon tends to be all business. This is the sign of the sea-goat, who can set his mind on climbing from the ocean to the top of the mountain - and make it there! It's a time for focus and certainty.

What is began under a Capricorn Moon can progress exactly as planned, and reach the intended goal. This does not happen quickly or easily, but you will likely find yourself with the resources to make it happen. If you are setting a goal, with great determination and a healthy dose of patience this is the time to get going. If you goal is unclear in any way, you are not prepared to plan and follow those plans meticulously, or are a bit uncertain of the whole thing - it will likely go no where under this Moon.

There is a serious, heavy feel to a Capricorn Moon. Compassion, empathy, and sensitivity are a bit harder to come by. It's often easier to cope with issues on a practical, financial, or logical level than an emotional one.

Capricorn Moon at a glance
- *Focus: determination, structure, plan*
- *Health: bones, joints*
- *Ruling Planet: Saturn*
- *Element: Earth*
- *Incense: musk*
- *Herbs: vervain, comfrey, nightshade*
- *Candle Colors: red, brown, dark green*
- *Manifest: business, goals, structuring, decisions*

Moon in Aquarius

Aquarius is the sign of the rebel; the free thinker. When the Moon falls in Aquarius the winds of change are blowing. This is the time to celebrate your eccentricities and let your hair down.

Whatever is began under an Aquarian Moon is highly unlikely to turn out as planned, or as expected. It's the time for breaking free of repression, difficult circumstances, someone else's influence - anything you wish to break free from. However, if you are looking to begin something for stabilization or structuring you're likely in for an unpleasant surprise if you begin it under this Moon.

The Aquarius Moon can strike a cord of rebellion in the meekest among us. It's not the best time for seeking cooperation in situations where people are at odds. However it is also a time of connections, so it can be excellent for forming friendships, and networks when there is a solid common ground.

Aquarius Moon at a Glance
- *Focus: change, freedom, connection*
- *Health: circulation, ankles and calves*
- *Ruling Planets: Uranus and Saturn*
- *Element: Air*
- *Incense: frankincense*
- *Herbs: lavender, mace, mint*
- *Candle Colors: azure, electric blue, light blue*
- *Manifest: freedom, seeking change, friendships*

Moon in Pisces

Pisces has a reputation as the most spiritual sign. In reality, the entire Zodiac relates to spirituality, but Pisces is by far the most open to the unseen. When the Moon is here, it's time to focus on anything and everything that isn't definitive or solid.

Things began under a Pisces Moon tend to grow and spread quickly as this is an extremely fertile sign. However, they lack focus and definition. It's the time to strive for openness, and emotional or spiritual growth and experience. If what you are seeking is within the realms of creativity, imagination, or the intangible side of reality this is the perfect Moon. However, if you set goals and make plans now, they will likely be lost or evolve into something altogether different.

The Pisces Moon makes people tend toward nostalgia, empathy, imagination, and flexibility. There is a contemplative, wandering, feeling to this Moon. It's a time when anything seems possible, yet nothing seems certain.

Pisces Moon at a Glance
- Focus : openness, vision, imagination
- Health: lymphatic system, feet
- Ruling Planets: Neptune, Jupiter
- Element: Water
- Incense: carnation
- Herbs: anise, eucalyptus, water lily
- Candle Colors: lavender, sea green, pearl
- Manifest: dreams, visions, creativity, release

Moon In Aries

The first sign of the Zodiac, Aries is the pioneer. This is the appropriate time for things involving leadership, new beginnings, physical strength, and courage. If are fighting a battle (hopefully not literally), this Moon is the time to make your move.

Whatever is initiated under Aries Moon has a quality of speed. If you are looking to the future, embarking on a long journey, or beginning projects requiring a long-term commitment, it's best to avoid this Moon. It's about short-term goals, quick action, and high energy.

There is a feeling of impatience in the air, and tempers run a bit hot when the Moon is passing through Aries. It's not the time to bring up sore subjects, or have heart-to-heart talks. It can be the time to put your foot down, or take on something you haven't found the courage for.

Aries Moon At A Glance
- *Focus: strength, vitality, energy*
- *Health: head, and face*
- *Ruling Planet: Mars*
- *Element: Fire*
- *Metal: Iron*
- *Incense: dragon's blood*
- *Herbs: fennel, cumin, wormwood*
- *Candle Colors: burgundy, scarlet, red, crimson, orange*
- *Manifest: authority, leadership, personal power*

Moon In Taurus

Taurus is the sign of the Zodiac most closely associated with our Mother Earth. This is the time for seeking grounding, stability and patience. The Taurus Moon solidifies and manifests. It is well suited for anything of the physical and material world.

Things began under a Taurus Moon, develop slowly. Quick result and instant gratification aren't likely under this Moon. It's a time of building, gradually and carefully. Begin things you intend to last, to slowly build and strengthen; start well planned, long-term projects.

The Taurus Moon whispers "slowly but surely".... It brings a heightened interest in creature comforts, anything soothing, and an eye on the future. It's not the time to launch into high energy or fast-paced activities. This is a time of steady progress towards goals, while finding the most scenic route to get there.

Taurus Moon At A Glance
- *Focus: grounding, patience, stability*
- *Health: neck and throat*
- *Ruling Planet: Venus*
- *Element: Earth*
- *Metal: Copper*
- *Incense: rose*
- *Herbs: cardamom, oak moss, lotus*
- *Candle Colors: jade, emerald, pink, turquoise, sapphire*
- *Manifest: money, grounding, the physical plane*

Moon in Gemini

The notoriously fickle sign of Gemini tends to be here, there, and everywhere. When it is host to the Moon, everything gets just a bit busier. This is a time of exploration, intriguing ideas, and seemingly endless details. It's the perfect time for multi-tasking and communication oriented activities.

Anything began under a Gemini Moon gets a bit scattered, and exists in a constant state of evolution. It certainly isn't the time to pull yourself together, put the blinders on and focus straight ahead. It's best to begin open-ended projects, tentative ventures, make the transition from wrapping-it-up to starting something new.

Curiosity fills the air, ideas flit around like little sprites, and everything unfamiliar becomes fascinating. We communicate well under a Gemini Moon, not only through words but also through the subtleties of thought, action and symbolism.

Gemini Moon at a Glance
- *Focus: learn, think, evolve*
- *Health: arms, hands, and lungs*
- *Ruling Planet: Mercury*
- *Element: Air*
- *Incense: citron*
- *Herbs: dill, parsley, lavender*
- *Candle Colors: yellow, mauve, green*
- *Manifest: communication, dissolving, expansion*

Moon In Cancer

In Cancer, the Moon is coming home, to revisit her own sign, under her own rulership. She beckons us to come home as well. All domestic matters come to the forefront under a Cancer Moon. This is a time to focus on home and hearth; heart and soul.

Things began under a Cancer Moon have a gentle, fluid quality. It's an excellent time for most planting (Waxing Moon), as this is the most fertile sign of the Zodiac. It's not a time to seek challenge, or make a dramatic push. This is a time to tend to the things that really matter, those you wish to nurture with loving care.

Cancer Moon often means a visit to the therapist - whether it be a professional's office, the shoulder of a good friend, or the bank of a gentle stream. This is a time of experiencing, releasing, and embracing emotions all to often buried beneath the surface.

Cancer Moon at a Glance
- *Focus: home, family, heart*
- *Health: stomach and chest*
- *Ruling Planet: Moon*
- *Element: water*
- *Incense: gardenia*
- *Herbs: Moonwort, clary sage, lemon balm*
- *Candle Colors : white, silver, amber*
- *Manifest: home, water, loved ones, emotions, fertility*

Moon In Leo

Proud, fiery Leo is ruled by the Sun. When the Moon falls in the sign of the Sun, a power boost is certain. This is a time for creativity and celebration. Anything intended to make an impact, or put on a show will thrive and flourish.

Thing began under a Leo Moon tend to take center stage. It's not the time to hesitate. Whatever you do will stand a better chance of success if you do it with enthusiasm. If you've been working up to a situation where you need to make a brazen move - Leo Moon is you chance.

There is a playful, showy, light-hearted feel to a Leo Moon. Everything seems a little dull without a nice, dramatic flair. However, we must not take ourselves too seriously, or this bright spot in the month can quickly turn dark. Pride becomes much more vulnerable, and fiercely guarded than you may realize - until it is wounded.

Leo Moon At A Glance
Focus: creativity, confidence, self-expression
Health: heart and spine
Ruling Planet: Sun
Element: Fire
Metal: Gold
Incense: sandalwood
Herbs: cinnamon, juniper, mistletoe
Candle Colors: gold, orange, yellow
Manifest: power, authority, creativity, wealth

Moon In Virgo

Virgo is known as the sign of efficiency and practicality. Use the Moon's passage through Virgo to set things straight. This is the perfect time for matters of health and wellness, organization, simplification, scheduling, or tending to details.

Things began under the discriminating Virgo Moon tend to become an exercise in the search for perfection. If you are starting a project that you need to keep on schedule and work out every glitch as it comes up - this is the time to begin. If you are seeking a bit more flexibility, giving little attention to planning, or intending to work sporadically in a stop-and-go fashion, this isn't the ideal time.

While the Moon is in Virgo you may notice a dip in morale. Moods tend to be heavy, and many people slip into a downcast or highly critical state. Virgo is the fault-finder, remember, it's a time meant for seeking improvement, not simply focusing on the need for it.

Virgo Moon At A Glance
- *Focus: improvement, simplification, purification*
- *Health: nervous system, intestines*
- *Ruling Planet: Mercury*
- *Element: Earth*
- *Incense: Patchouli*
- *Herbs: rosemary, silver root, vervain*
- *Candle Colors: dark gray, dark orange, dark blue*
- *Manifest: health, purification, employment, pets*

MOON IN LIBRA

Libra - the Scales of Justice; the sign of romance. The Libra Moon is about balance, about looking at the other side. Whether that is the other side in an argument, the other half of a relationship - the 'other' needs a little more attention under this Moon.

Things began while the Moon is traveling through Libra tend to be changeable, progress with an air of gracefulness, and stall frequently as factors fall out of balance. If you are beginning something intended to be peaceful, in the pursuit of justice, focus on aesthetics or flow harmoniously this is the time. Taking on challenges, or making big changes are best left for another time.

The Libra Moon seems to bring out the romantic, the artist, or the socialite in everyone. Other people become more fascinating, and we are a bit more aware of the beauty (or lack thereof) in our surroundings.

LIBRA MOON AT A GLANCE
- *Focus: balance, beauty, justice*
- *Health: kidneys, spine, lower back*
- *Ruling Planet: Venus*
- *Element: Air*
- *Incense: rose*
- *Herbs: thyme, catnip, mugwort*
- *Candle Colors: emerald green, deep blue, magenta*
- *Manifest: justice, balance, karma, legal troubles*

Moon In Scorpio

Scorpio is the most intense sign of the Zodiac, producing he most intense Moon transits. This is the time of power - building it, using it, or being confronted with the power of other people/events.

Anything began under a Scorpio Moon takes on a depth, intensity and power of its own. They can be challenging to control, and even more difficult to end (or re-start if you are initiating an ending) if you should change your mind. If you are seeking ultimate reality - the good the bad and the ugly -this is the time. It's not the time for hesitant beginnings, or seeking a predictable, controllable defined path.

While the Moon is passing through Scorpio, she stirs some pretty powerful emotions. People struggling with emotional problems such as depression, or obsession often find it intensifying under a Scorpio Moon. In fact, we are all prone to run face first into our most difficult emotions bubbling to the surface.

Scorpio Moon at a Glance
- *Focus: power, depth, intensity*
- *Health: bodily elimination systems, reproductive organs*
- *Ruling Planets: Mars and Pluto*
- *Element: Water*
- *Incense: frankincense*
- *Herbs: valerian, ginger, basil*
- *Candle Colors: black, brown, crimson red*
- *Manifest: power, sex, transformation*

Moon In Sagittarius

Sagittarius is the sign of new experiences and exotic places. When the Moon passes through Sagittarius she opens doors, and opens minds. This is the time to experiment and experience. Try something different.

What is began under a Sagittarius Moon can take off like wildfire. Quick action, growth, and continuous expansion are inherent to this placement. It's a good time for beginning things of a financial nature, or anything aimed at enriching your life. If you are seeking predictability, controllable growth, or a cautious approach it's best not to begin under this Moon.

The playful Sagittarius Moon often draws us into her adventurous spirit. Sagittarius is also a sign of belief. It can be a time of great educational, spiritual, or philosophical expansion. It can also lead to some heated debates when a nerve is touched relating to what one deeply believes.

Sagittarius Moon At A Glance
- *Focus: expansion, belief, experience*
- *Health: liver, thighs*
- *Ruling Planet: Jupiter*
- *Element: Fire*
- *Incense: carnation*
- *Herbs: clove, sage, pennyroyal*
- *Candle Colors: purple, red, royal blue*
- *Manifest: travel, far away people, truth, expansion*

Additional Resources

Even though we have come to the end of this journey, remember that the journey continues every 29 day Lunar cycle. The Moon, since the dawn of time has kept her promise to return night after night. Even when we can't see her, she is there. Ever loyal, ever inviting, ever ready to aid you in manifesting the life you seek.

This book introduced Moon cosmology that is derived from many lands, beliefs and wisdom traditions. To continue your studies I invite you to visit my website, erickdupree.com and sign up for my news letter. I am also very accessible by email, at erick@erickdupree.com

If you are seeking additional readings I recommend the following:

The Spiral Dance by Starhawk
WitchCrafting by Phyllis Curott
Moon Magic by Dione Fortune (Fiction)
Sea Priestess by Dione Fortune (Fiction)
Alone in Her Presence by Erick DuPree
Making Magic of Your Life by T. Thorn Coyle
The Deep Heart of Witchcraft by David Salisbury
Astrology of the Moon by Amy Herring
Moon Signs by Donna Cunningham
The Astrological Moon by Hayden Paul

The journey has really just begun!

Bibliography

Adler, Margot. Drawing Down the Moon. Boston: Beacon Press, 1986. (Revised and expanded edition).

Ann, Martha and Dorothy Myers Imel. Goddesses in World Mythology. Santa Barbara, CA: ABC-Clio, 1993.

Barner-Barry, Carol. Contemporary Paganism: Minority Religions in a Majoritarian America. New York: Palgrave MacMillan, 2005.

Berger, Helen A. A Community of Witches: Contemporary Neo-Paganism and Witchcraft in the United States. Columbia, South Carolina: University of South Carolina Press, 1999.

Berger, Helen A., ed. Witchcraft and Magic: Contemporary North America. Philadelphia: University of Pennsylvania Press, 2005.

Berger, Pamela. The Goddess Obscured: Transformation of the Grain Protectress to Saint. Boston: Beacon Press, 1985.

Blain, Jenny, Douglas Ezzy, and Graham Harvey, ed. Researching Paganisms. Walnut Creek, CA: AltaMira Press, 2004.

Bonewits, P.E.I. Real Magic. Berkeley, CA: Creative Arts Book Company, 1971.

Budapest, Z. The Holy Book of Women's Mysteries. Oakland: Susan B. Anthony Coven 1, 1989.

Cabot, Laurie, with Tom Cowan. Power of the Witch: A Witches Guide to Her Craft. Baltimore: Penguin Books, 1989.

Christ, Carol P. She Who Changes: Re-Imagining the Divine in the World. New York: Palgrave MacMillan, 2003.

Clifton, Chas S. Her Hidden Children: The Rise of Wicca and Paganism in America. New York: Altamira Press, 2006.

Clifton, Chas S. and Graham Harvey. The Paganism Reader. New York: Routledge, 2004.

Coyle, T. Thorn. Evolutionary Witchcraft. New York: Penguin, 2004.

Cunningham, Scott. Wicca: A Guide for the Solitary Practitioner. Llewellyn Publications, 1992.

Davy, Barbara Jane. Introduction to Pagan Studies. New York: Altamira Press, 2006.

De Angeles, Ly, Emma Restall Orr, and Thom van Dooren. Pagan Visions for a Sustainable Future. St. Paul, MN: Llewellyn Press, 2005.

Ehrenreich, Barbara, and Dierdre English. Witches, Midwives and Nurses. New York: Feminist Press, 1963.

Eller, Cynthia, Living in the Lap of the Goddess. New York: Crossroad Publishing, 1993.

The Feminist Spiritual Community of Portland, Maine. Keep Simple Ceremonies. Astarte Shell Press, 1995.
Gadon, Elinor W. The Once and Future Goddess: A Symbol For Our Time. San Francisco: Harper & Row, 1989.

Gardner, Gerald B. Witchcraft Today. New York: Citadel Press, 1955.

Gimbutas, Marija. The Goddesses and Gods of Old Europe: Myths and Cult Images. Berkeley: University of California Press, 1982.

Griffin, Wendy, ed. Daughters of the Goddess: Studies of Healing, Identity, and Empowerment. Walnut Creek, California: Altamira Press, 2000.

Harris, Judith Grove. "The Challenges of Growth in Contemporary Pagan Community." Independent Study, Harvard Divinity School, 1995.

Harrow, Judy, Spiritual Mentoring: A Pagan Guide. Toronto: ECW Press, 2002.

Harrow, Judy. Wicca Covens: How to Start and Organize Your Own. Secaucus, NJ: Citadel Press, 1999.

Harvey, Graham. Contemporary Paganism: Living People, Speaking Earth. Washington Square, NY: New York University Press, 1997.

Higginbotham, Joyce and River. Paganism: An Introduction to Earth-Centered Religions. St. Paul, MN: Llewellyn Press, 2002.

Hutton, Ronald. The Triumph of the Moon: A History of Modern Pagan Witchcraft. Oxford: Oxford University Press, 1999.

Luhrmann, T. M. Persuasions of the Witch's Craft: Ritual Magic in Contemporary England. Cambridge: Harvard University Press, 1989.

Magliocco, Sabina. Witching Culture: Folklore and Neo-Paganism in America. Philadelphia: University of Pennsylvania Press, 2004.

NightMare, M. Macha. Pagan Pride: Honoring the Craft and Culture of the Earth and Goddess. New York: Kensington Publishing, 2003.

Northrup, Lesley A. Ritualizing Women: Patterns of Spirituality. Cleveland: The Pilgrim Press, 1997.

Paige, Anthony. Rocking the Goddess: Campus Wicca for the Student Practitioner. New York: Kensington Publishing, 2002.

Paris, Ginette. Pagan Meditations: The Worlds of Aphrodite, Artemis, and Hestia. Dallas: Spring Publications, Inc., 1986.

Pike, Sarah M. Earthly Bodies, Magical Selves: Contemporary Pagans and the Search for Community. Berkeley, California: University of California Press, 2001.

Pike, Sarah M. New Age and Neopagan Religions in America. New York: Columbia University Press, 2004.

Purkiss, Diane. The Witch in History: Early Modern and Twentieth-century Representations. London: Routledge, 1996.

Reis, Elizabeth. Manifestationbound: Women and Witchcraft in America. Wilmington: Scholarly Resources Inc., 1998.

Starhawk. The Spiral Dance: A Rebirth of the Ancient Religion of the Great Goddess. San Francisco: Harper & Row, 1979.

Starhawk, Diane Baker, and Anne Hill. Circle Round: Raising Children in Goddess Traditions. New York: Bantam, 2001.

Starhawk, M. Macha NightMare, and the Reclaiming Collective. The Pagan Book of Living and Dying: Practical Rituals, Prayers, Blessings, and Meditations on Crossing Over. San Francisco: Harper San Francisco, 1997.

Streep, Peg. Sanctuaries of the Goddess. Boston: Little, Brown and Company, 1994.

Walker, Barbara. The Woman's Encyclopedia of Myths and Secrets. San Francisco: Harper & Row, 1983.

York, Michael. Pagan Theology: Paganism as a World Religion. New York: New York
University Press, 2003.

IMAGES

All images are used with permission, are Common Use, or are the property of the author

Cover	ERICK DUPREE, ORIGINAL ART
6	THE MOON TAROT CARD, RIDER-WAITE TAROT DECK
22	LUNAR PHASES, © 2000 CAROLYN MYERS
41	AUTHOR'S ALTAR
56	AUTHOR'S LUNAR JOURNAL
68	MOON WATER AND LUNAR BOWL, AUTHOR
28	WAXING, WAINING, ALIVE © MICHAEL BATISTES
92	AUTHORS TAROT JOURNAL
114	THE MOON, ALPHONSE MUCHA
123	TRIPLE GODDESS, ©2014 STEPHANIE BLACKHEART
134	CHANG-O iSTOCK PHOTO
142	IXCHEL THE GODDESS ORACLE DECK
154	DIANA CLAUDE BOUCHER
175	MOON SKETCH, AUTHOR
194	MOON PHASES AND SEASONS CLIP ART
202	ASTROLOGY CHART iSTOCK PHOTO
216	LADY IN THE MOON ARTIST UNKNOWN

LUNAR NOTES
13 MOONS OF OPPORTUNITY!

NOTES

Notes

Notes

NOTES

NOTES

NOTES

NOTES

Notes

NOTES

Notes

Notes

NOTES

NOTES

About the Author

Erick DuPree has a unique writer's voice that blends many wisdom traditions and draws inspiration and spirit from the Goddess, Earth, and our Divine Immanence.

Erick's studies have included working within Reclaiming Collective, WitchCamps, Soul Work with T. Thorn Coyle, as well as mentoring under Rev. Kim Crawford-Harvie of Arlington Street Church: Boston. Today he studies Occult Magick with Ivo Dominquez, Jr. Tantra with Douglas Brooks, and maintains a rigorous zazen practice at Village Zendo, in NYC. Erick trains with Jillian Pranksy in Restorative Yoga, teaches Dharma Paganism with Yeshe Rabbit Matthews, and is trained in various modalities of energy work including Chakra Balancing and Reiki.

As writer, Erick is most known for Alone in Her Presence, a blog - turned book - turned column, now hosted on Patheos.com where he writes about knowing Goddess as the Healing Vessel. He is author of *Alone In Her Presence: Meditations on the Goddess*, and the anthology, *Finding Masculine in Goddess' Spiral: Men in Ritual, Community and Service to the Goddess*, by Immanion Press.

He is currently working on his next title, The Healing Vessel: An Earth Goddess Devotional, by Circle Within Press (2015). Erick has contributed to numerous anthologies and national publications on diverse topics including surviving sexual trauma, race relations, adaptive leadership, and children's faith development.

He lives in Philadelphia, PA.

www.ingramcontent.com/pod-product-compliance
Lightning Source LLC
Chambersburg PA
CBHW070733160426
43192CB00009B/1428